Moving to Europe
as an Expat

MOVING TO EUROPE AS AN EXPAT

Step-by-step guide on how to move to Europe, get a job, buy a house, travel around the world and acquire European citizenship

Copyright (c) 2021 Kyryl Lashun
All rights reserved

Moving to Europe as an Expat ISBNs:

978-83-8273-218-4 Paperback
979-87-5694-953-7 KDP ISBN

Special thanks to:

Book cover: https://en.99designs.nl/profiles/boja
Typesetting: Predrag Markovic - www.markovicpredrag.com
Design: Yaroslav Kholod
Proofreading: Rihard Thrift, http://english-editing.nl

CONTENTS

Moving to Europe as an Expat

Executive summary 7
What this book is about 11

PART I: WHY 15

Why everyone needs to move 17
What it takes to move to the EU, get a job, buy a house and get EU citizenship 27

PART II: WHERE 31

Europe or North America? 33

PART III: HOW 39

Legal reasons for moving abroad 41
MBA application 53
Negotiating your scholarship 65
Confirmation and preparing for the move 73

PART IV: FIRST YEAR 78

Registering at the municipality, residence card,
bank account, GP, insurance 79
Accommodation 85
Living costs 89
Allowances 99
MBA 103

Traveling in Europe..107
Search year visa 113
Useful tips for a newbie 115

PART V: GETTING A JOB 117

Where to look for a job and how to succeed.. 119
CV 127
Interview 131
Salary and contract conditions 137
First year in the company 141
How to succeed in the corporate world.. 143

PART VI: BUYING A HOUSE.. 145

How to choose a house..147
How to apply for a mortgage 155
Bidding..159
House inspection 165
Signing a contract 167
Moving in, renovation, settling down.. 171
Tax return..177

PART VII: PERMANENT RESIDENCE OR PASSPORT...................................179

Criteria to apply for permanent residence (PR) or citizenship.................. 181
Integration exams... 185
Preparing the documents.. 189
Decision and naturalization ceremony..193

PART VIII: WHAT'S NEXT..195

Now you are a European citizen, what's next? 197

EXECUTIVE SUMMARY

Turning a dream into a plan and executing it

This plan is based on my personal experience in the Netherlands. Please check the regulations of your target country in detail.

To move to Europe and get a job you need to complete several steps:

1. **Figure out which of the legal reasons works best for you:**
   - Study visa
   - Highly skilled migrant visa
   - Partner visa

2. Depending on the reason you need to **apply for a Master's or Ph.D. program, apply for a job** or your partner needs to arrange the documents for you.

3. Then you will **get a temporary entrance visa valid for 3 months.** This visa can be substituted for a temporary residence permit (depending on the reason for your stay).

4. You also need to **arrange accommodation and a minimum amount of money**—if this amount is not enough for the length of your stay, **figure out how you can get additional income** by, for example, working remotely (if you have a study visa).

5. If the reason for your entry was to study, when you complete your studies you need to **apply for a search year visa,** which allows you to work temporarily and **start looking for a permanent job.**

6. You also need to familiarize yourself with the tax system, so you can, for example, **get the tax back** on your tuition fee later or **get a 30% ruling** (if you were hired from abroad).

7. Normally, a first-year contract is temporary, and then it can be extended to **a permanent contract**. After working for about 2 years you can consider **applying for a mortgage and buying a house.**

8. Once you have a job, and a house, it is time to **relax and travel around.**

9. After 3-4 years of staying in the country, you can start **preparation for the integration exams.**

10. Normally **after 5 years you can apply for a permanent residence or a passport**. After getting this, you are no longer dependent on your employer for a visa and can stay in the country even if you lose your job. In addition, a passport gives you all the rights of other EU citizens including the right to live and work in any EU country.

11. **Now it is time to think about what you want to do next.** Do you want to continue a corporate job, or do you want to start your own business? Do you want to follow your passion and volunteer, dedicate your time to supporting an NGO, or do you prefer a quiet family life with enough time for your hobbies and traveling?

Executive summary

It is another chapter of your life, and maybe one day I will write a book about it. For now – first things first – let's discuss how to move to Europe and start executing your plan!

WHAT THIS BOOK IS ABOUT

This book is a practical step-by-step guide on how to:
- ☑ Move to Europe
- ☑ Get a job
- ☑ Buy a house
- ☑ Travel the world
- ☑ Acquire European citizenship (if you want to)

Each chapter explains one of the steps in detail. Combined, they provide a template, which you can fill with your own circumstances, and successfully achieve your objective.

On the last pages of the book, you will find a link to my website, where you can ask additional questions. I promise to answer as many of them as I can.

Before we start, here is my story.

Six years ago, I lived in Ukraine, had a middle-level job, and nothing to look forward to. My life was ok, but it was life in a box.

I lived on the same street from the age of four until I was thirty. I went to the school across the street, graduated from the same university as my parents, and got a similar job.

I was just polishing the mold made for me.

All I was supposed to do is to follow the given path until I get old and retire. My remaining years were to be filled not with the memories of my wonderful life, but rather with complaints and bitterness.

My world was small, my dreams were small, and I myself was small. It was tiring to be this person.

I had a map on the wall, and sometimes in the evening I looked at it and read the names of different cities: Tokyo, Marrakesh, Copenhagen, Amsterdam, London, Paris, New York... They sounded like a promise of a different life. This life existed for many people, but I didn't know how to become one of them.

Slowly my career progressed, so I travelled to Europe several times and loved it. I loved the windy streets of Copenhagen, the beautiful canals of Amsterdam, music on the streets of Paris, and the smell of the seafood and salty wind of Barcelona. I felt that I belonged to all those places. But I also felt like an unwelcome guest, as I needed a visa and a long list of documents to visit them just for a few days.

Whenever I arrived home, I had to fit back into my mold and crawl through the gray days, one resembling another. Yes, I had friends, family, and hobbies, but despite this, I felt like a dog on a chain.

New life was so inviting. It was tempting to become a new person living in a new place, to speak a different language, to see the world, to become somebody new.

I kept thinking: at least once in your life you need to escape from the limitations of your given circumstances and go somewhere else, far away, to truly understand who you are and where you belong. Maybe then you will go back. It is ok to go back. But then you will go back because you chose to, not because you didn't dare to leave the path defined by your parents or circumstances.

One evening, after a couple of glasses of port, I made an appointment for a GMAT test and applied to a one-year MBA program at two European business schools.

I was shocked when both accepted me.

But the tuition fee was too high, and I had almost zero savings.

I told them that I needed to postpone the MBA for one year. Deep in my heart, I thought that this was just a nice way to say that I had postponed it forever. But, thanks to my stubbornness and persistence I proceeded with my preparation.

One year later I flew to the Netherlands to join a full-time MBA program with just three thousand euros in my pocket. I still had to pay 80% of my tuition fee. And just renting a room was going to cost at least 700 euros per month.

I started with zero. I bluffed it—and it was not that hard. You just need to take the first step. And then one more step, and the next one. Everything else will take care of itself.

Where am I now?

I completed my MBA and paid the tuition.

I got a job and am currently working in the headquarters of one of the top-10 Dutch multinationals in Amsterdam.

I also bought a 3-story house with a roof terrace in Utrecht, a beautiful city 20 minutes from Amsterdam, the cycling capital of the world.

I completed integration exams and acquired Dutch nationality, which means that I am now an EU citizen, and can live and work anywhere in the European Union, as well as enjoy visa-free access to 177 countries.

I traveled across the globe, flying at least 2-3 times a month, both for business and pleasure, and have visited most of the cities on my list, including New York, Tokyo, London, Paris, Madrid, Barcelona, Vienna, Singapore, Taipei, Saigon, Bangkok, Seoul, Hong Kong, Chicago, Lisbon, Berlin, Zurich, Oslo, Stockholm, Helsinki, Milan, Vienna, Budapest, Prague, Marrakesh, and many others.

Now, six years later, I am writing these lines while on vacation in Greece, on the beautiful island of Rhodes with blue sky and plenty of salty water which they call the Mediterranean Sea.

I am writing for those who also want to build a new life or are just curious to experience life elsewhere for a while. Maybe you are in the same situation as I was six years ago. Maybe you want to move, want to start a new chapter, want to study or work in Europe or even become an EU citizen, but do not know how to start or what it takes. The purpose of this book is to provide a step-by-step practical guide on how to do it, as well as to give you some inspiration along the way.

You do not need anything to start. I, myself, started with zero.
You only need to dare to take the first step. And then the next one.

Until you get where you want to be.

Ready? Let's go!

PART I: **WHY**

WHY EVERYONE NEEDS TO MOVE

At least once in your life, you need to leave your hometown and go somewhere else. Only this move will give you a perspective and serve as an observation point, from where you can evaluate your past and decide your future.

Where do you want to live? Who do you want to be? What do you want to do?

It could be that you will decide to go back and stay the same person. That's ok, because then it is your choice. Or maybe you will go far away and become somebody else. Transform from a clerk in a small local company to a leader of the division in a large multinational in London. Or become an entrepreneur, create a new product and change the world.

To become somebody new, you need to depart from your old self. Physically.

There is a concept, developed by Joseph Campbell, called "Hero's Journey". Campbell says that all narratives share a fundamental structure. All the stories are about somebody who left their hometown to travel the world, slay the dragon to meet their true self, define their character, and shape it with new experiences and difficulties that they had to overcome on their journey.

When I listen to the stories of other expats, most of them are a 90% match to a Hero's Journey template. Therefore, there is a high chance that your journey will also unfold similarly.

This is the only "impractical" part of the book, so feel free to skip it, if you only need facts.

The journey goes like this:

DEPARTURE

1. The Call to Adventure

The hero begins in a situation of normality from which some information is received that acts as a call to head off into the unknown.

For example, you realize that there is a job or a study opportunity abroad, but you do not have enough money or guts to take it. You want it and fear it at the same time. That's the call to adventure.

2. Refusal of the Call

Often when the call is given, the future hero first refuses to heed it. This may be from a sense of duty or obligation, fear, insecurity, a sense of inadequacy, or any of a range of reasons that work to hold the person in their current circumstances.

I postponed my MBA for a year because it was such an alien idea for me at that time to leave my hometown and move abroad to the unknown. Your family, financial situation, or personal insecurity might hold you back. It is helpful to know that it is a standard situation and a part of the journey. Most people who moved abroad experienced it. Just carry on as if nothing is holding you back.

3. Supernatural Aid

Once the hero has committed to the quest, consciously or unconsciously, their guide and magical helper appears or becomes known. Often, this supernatural mentor will present the hero with one or more talismans or artifacts that will aid them later in their quest.

In my case, I didn't have enough savings to pay for my education and life abroad. But magic started happening once I committed to the journey. The same will happen with you. When you decide, parts of the puzzle will start coming together to make it work.

4. The Crossing of the First Threshold

This is the point where the hero crosses into the field of adventure, leaving the known limits of their world and venturing into an unknown and dangerous realm where the rules and limits are unknown.

Just buy a ticket, get to the airport and board the plane. Get some wine, watch a movie or take a nap! The pilot will do the job for you. Crossing the line is easy. Do not look to the horizon, as it will only make you feel dizzy. Look one step ahead and focus on what you need to do NOW.

5. Belly of the Whale

The belly of the whale represents the final separation from the hero's known world and self. By entering this stage, the person shows a willingness to undergo a metamorphosis. When first entering the stage the hero may encounter a minor danger or setback.

When you start living abroad, you might experience isolation, loneliness and fear. You will need to adjust to the new culture, climate, and food. But trust me: humans can adjust to any circumstances. And it can be very exciting. Every day is brand new, and you feel like a new person. In the modern world, there are not so many real threats, especially if you are moving to a developed European country.

Enjoy the ride, eat well, sleep enough, take vitamins, and exercise daily. It is going to be alright!

INITIATION

6. The Road of Trials

The road of trials is a series of tests that the hero must undergo to begin the transformation. Often the hero fails one or more of these tests, which often occur in threes. Eventually, the hero will overcome these trials and move on to the next step.

You will run out of money. You will struggle to get a job. You will miss your hometown, family, and times when life was easy. But you won't get stronger by following the flow; you only get stronger by overcoming the circumstances. Hard choices = easy life. Easy choices = hard life. The easiest thing in life is to sit on the couch, drink beer and watch Netflix. But it will not get you to a happy place in the long term.

7. The Meeting with the Goddess

This is where the hero gets items given to them that will help them in the future.

You will meet new friends. You will get temporary jobs that will pay for your rent and food. You will get unexpected emails from recruiters. Even though you will only connect the dots later, events at the beginning of your journey will be stepping-stones to your future successes. When I look back at some failures and rejections I had in the past, I think: 'thank God things went this way'. There will be plenty of gifts on your journey. Talk to people. Knock on as many doors as you can. And things will start happening.

8. Woman as the Temptress

In this step, the hero faces those temptations, often of a physical or pleasurable nature, that may lead them to abandon or stray from their quest.

In one year, you will settle down in the new country. You will start enjoying it. And when there are opportunities somewhere else you will be reluctant to move. But you need to move: to a new town, to a new company, to a new social group. You should have a clear sense of direction but be flexible and opportunistic about how you going to get there.

9. Atonement with the Father/Abyss

In this step, the hero must confront and be initiated by whatever holds the ultimate power in their life. In many myths and stories, this is the father or a father figure who has life and death power. This is the center point of the journey. All the previous steps have been moving into this place, all that follow will move out from it. Although this step is most frequently symbolized by an encounter with a male entity, it does not have to be a male—just someone or something with incredible power.

Well, probably your father is far away. Your metaphorical father or the main obstacle in the new country is getting a job, so you have a legal reason to stay and an income to survive. Some of my friends were looking for a job for several months. Most of them suffered and were in doubt whether they would manage to confront the abyss (job search) and survive. But all of them did. It is just a matter of persistence. And conquering this obstacle brings multiple gifts. Now all my friends bought houses and cars, and traveled extensively. They also became better people: more confident, energized, positive, and with an optimistic outlook on the future. A job is a temporary answer and at a certain point, you will challenge it. But getting a job at the beginning of your journey solves many important problems.

10. Apotheosis

This is the point of realization in which a greater understanding is achieved. Armed with this new knowledge and perception, the hero is resolved and ready for the more difficult part of the adventure.

When you get a job and buy a house, you suddenly realize that not much has changed. You got used to your new life, you got stronger, but ultimate freedom has not been achieved yet. You are still waiting to apply for your passport and hope that it will change something (it won't). But somehow you start thinking: is this it?

11. The Ultimate Boon

The ultimate boon is the achievement of the goal of the quest. It is what the hero went on the journey to get. All the previous steps serve to prepare and purify the hero for this step since in many myths the boon is something transcendent like the elixir of life itself, or a plant that supplies immortality, or the holy grail.

Normally this is when you get a passport and become an EU citizen. Now you can travel to 175 countries without a visa and live and work in any EU country. But after 5-6 years living in the country, it is not a great breakthrough, because you feel that you deserved it anyway.

Now you start thinking about what's next and making plans. Don't get me wrong, it is great to get an EU passport, but it is just the beginning of another journey.

RETURN

12. Refusal of the Return

Having found bliss and enlightenment in the other world, the hero may not want to return to the ordinary world to bestow the boon onto his fellow humans.

Have you achieved what you wanted? Or not? Or maybe you want something else now?

It all depends on your character. Some people feel very happy with their job, family and new life. Some move within Europe to begin a new adventure. Some seek financial freedom and start their business to stop selling their time and reporting to somebody.

Do you want to settle down and live a normal life, or you want to start another journey?

13. The Magic Flight

Sometimes the hero must escape with the boon if it is something that the gods have been jealously guarding. It can be just as adventurous and dangerous returning from the journey as it was to go on it.

After achieving your goal, you will have more questions, because determination and focus on your objective are now unemployed. Now you have an EU passport, where do you want to return to?

You missed 5-6 years of communication with friends in your home country, so it is difficult to catch up. You are still a bit of a foreigner in your new country, even though you have a passport. The difficulty with returning is based on the fact that there is no place to return to. Realizing this can be sad or inspiring, depending on how you choose to feel about it.

14. Freedom to Live

In this step, mastery leads to freedom from the fear of death, which in turn is the freedom to live. This is sometimes referred to as living in the moment, neither anticipating the future nor regretting the past.

After moving geographically, accumulating wealth, and building relationships you realize that the most important part of life was always hidden from you because it was right in front of you while you were looking somewhere else to find it: THIS MOMENT.

This moment is the only place where something happens. We always anticipate and plan it, but we rarely live it.

You learn how to be in the moment. You drop the idea of achievement, performance and optimization because it entails so much pressure, tension and anxiety that it disturbs the calmness of your happiness. Now you can just live, without any objective or strategy. In the here and now.

At this point, the hero's journey is completed. Now you know why you had to move: to become a hero!

Moving abroad is a line between your old and new life, between your old and new self. When you cross this line, you create an opportunity to define who you are, where you want to be, and what you want to do.

And then there are many more lines. Everyone can see them. But only heroes can cross them.

WHAT IT TAKES TO MOVE TO THE EU, GET A JOB, BUY A HOUSE AND GET EU CITIZENSHIP

Here's the map:

Step 1: Reason to stay. You need to decide what legal reason works best for you.

The most common reasons for expats are:
- Studying
- Work
- Partnership

Step 2: Apply for a job or educational program in your destination country. Your employer or university / business school will sponsor your visa.

Step 3: Mvv entrance visa. Your sponsor (employer, university, or your partner) needs to submit an application to get approval from the Immigration authorities for you. An mvv is a temporary entry visa that will be replaced with a (temporary) residence permit. You can apply for this permit when you arrive in the country and register at the municipality.

You cannot make an application for an mvv visa yourself. Somebody from your destination country needs to prove to the authorities that you have a legal reason to live in the country.

Step 3: Accommodation. When you get an mvv visa, you can start searching for accommodation, if this is not being arranged by the university or your future employer. When the accommodation is confirmed, you can book a ticket and start packing your luggage.

Step 4: Registering at the municipality. When you arrive at your destination country you need to register at the municipality. In the Netherlands, you need a rental agreement to do this. When you register at the municipality you get a BSN number that serves as your unique identifier for various organizations (e.g., tax authorities).

Step 5: Temporary residence card. After registering at the municipality, you need to get a residence card. In most cases, your sponsor (employer, or your partner) needs to apply for this. You can find the list of required documents on the website of the Immigration authorities. Later you can extend this residence card if you would like to get a search year visa (after finishing your studies).

Step 6: Allowances. While studying you won't get any income, so in some countries you qualify for a housing allowance or health insurance allowance. You can check the criteria and apply on the website of the tax authorities (use Google translate if you do not understand the local language). An allowance is a monthly payment from the tax authorities to cover the gap between your income and your basic needs (health insurance, rent, etc.) For example, in the Netherlands, minimal health insurance is around 90 euros a month. If you do not have any income, the tax office will transfer this amount to your account so you can pay for your insurance.

Step 7: Job search. If your primary reason for entering the country was to study, then after graduating you need to get an internship or directly look for a job.

Step 8: Travelling and enjoying life (approx. 2-3 years of staying in the new country). When you have a job (and it is still too early to look for a house) you can enjoy life and travel around.

Step 9: Buying a house. After working for 2-3 years it is time to buy a house. Buying a house has multiple advantages, so you should do it no matter whether you plan to stay long term or go back to your home country later.

Step 10: Tax return. In Europe, we pay a lot of tax, so it is important to get some of your tax back. There are several ways to do this. Read the next chapters to learn the details.

Step 11: Integration exams. After 4 years of staying in the country, you can consider preparing to apply for a permanent residence or even citizenship. To apply for this you need to complete integration exams.

Step 12: EU citizenship. After 5 years of staying in the country (at least in the Netherlands) you are eligible to apply for citizenship. Of course, it depends on the country, but for example, in the Netherlands, you only need a few documents and it takes around 1 year to get a decision and get invited to the ceremony.

Step 13: What's next? Mission complete; what's next?

PART II: **WHERE**

EUROPE OR NORTH AMERICA?

Well, of course, this is my personal opinion, so please take it with a pinch of salt. I haven't visited Canada, so I will compare Europe (more specifically the European Union) with the United States.

European Union

Europe is all about equality and basic social security for everyone. Higher social costs mean higher taxes and a less competitive economy (because social costs are high and disposing of redundant resources is expensive). Living in Europe is great, basic needs are covered, education and healthcare are cheap, and mortgages are affordable. It is difficult to get rich, but it is relatively easy to live a good life. Also, Europe is very diverse in terms of cultures, landscapes and climates, and has a great history and traditions. You can fly from the north (Stockholm) to the south (Malaga) in about 3 hours and be in a totally different environment. European cities are walkable, they have a nice vibe, there are thousands of theatres, museums and exhibitions, and it is intellectually pleasing to live here.

In general, if you look at the map, countries in northern Europe are the richest, but the climate there is bad, food is boring and people are more distant from each other. I am talking about Sweden, Norway, Finland, Denmark and the Netherlands. On the positive side, these are small nations that need to adjust to the rest of the world, so almost everyone speaks English.

Countries in the middle (Germany, France) are quite big, have a strong local culture, and mostly prefer to speak their own language, and therefore are less flexible to English-speaking expats. But they have strong economies, not necessarily in terms of quality, but definitely in terms of volume.

Finally, countries in the south (Spain, Portugal, Italy) have less money but have better food, better weather, and interactions between people are less formal. Ideally, you make money in the north and live in the south.

Pros of Europe

- High social security
- Easy to live an average life without too much effort (house, car, healthcare, education)
- Very safe
- Diversity of cultures
- Beautiful cities, deep historical roots

Cons

- Stagnating economy due to high social costs
- Difficult to get rich, less free capital and opportunities
- In many cases, you need to learn an additional language (but it can be a plus)

United States

The United States is a country of immigrants, where everyone speaks English, so it should be relatively easy to adjust and feel at home there. There is plenty of capital and opportunities, you can go as high as you can, and culture supports this ambition. Social costs are shifted from the government to the individual, resulting in a strong economy with plenty of start-ups and large corporations. The U.S. has a vast territory with different types of climate, so you can choose where to live: desert, beach, megalopolis, or snowy mountains.

With some exceptions, the United States is not a country where you can walk. Most of it is an endless road with one-story houses on each side. There are many nice restaurants but on average the quality of food is low.

Lastly, not everywhere is safe. There are areas of cities that you should not visit at night. Also it is possible to buy a gun, so you never know who has one.

Pros

- Plenty of capital and business opportunities
- Vast territory with diverse climate
- English-speaking country, so easy to adjust and become a part of a society

Cons

- Social security is not as high as in Europe
- There are places that are not safe
- Food is not great

- Culture is not as diverse as in Europe
- You need to accept life with very little walking possibilities, living in relative isolation (no neighborhood), and you also need to like the American vibe

There is no right or wrong choice. The U.S. is all about opportunities, but you must compromise on the vibe, security, and culture. Europe is cozy and vibrant, very diverse, with deep historical roots, but in terms of the lifestyle, it puts you in the (comfortable) middle. In Europe, you are also more likely to need to learn at least one additional language (though this is not necessarily a bad thing).

Before moving to Europe, I visited many countries, and then I also visited the city where my future university was located, just to feel what it would be like to live there. It felt good, so I moved, and never had any regrets. Later I went to the U.S. as well and felt that it was not a place where I wanted to live. But some of my friends felt differently, so the best advice is to visit the country before moving and try to imagine yourself living there. If it makes you feel excited, then move there; if not, visit another country, until you find the one you like. It is also about your priorities: are you comfortable with a guaranteed spot in the middle, or you are willing to take more risks and aim higher, accepting a more individualistic society and carrying a larger social security risk on your shoulders?

Regarding Europe, you probably want to start your career somewhere in the north or in the middle, where the economy is more developed, social security is higher and companies and culture are more international. But maybe at a certain point, you want to live in a better climate, eat better food, chat and laugh with neighbors and enjoy a more vibrant society & landscape. If so, then you should move to the south, where the economy is weaker, but the vibe, the food, and the atmosphere are much better! And hey, why would you care about the economy if you can eat tapas & drink Rioja every day?

PART III: **HOW**

LEGAL REASONS FOR MOVING ABROAD

We will focus on the 3 main reasons to move to the EU and apply for a residence permit:

1. Family
2. Study
3. Work

In each of these cases, you need a sponsor for your application – somebody who will initiate and sponsor it.

As an example, we will use the process for the Netherlands. You need to check the regulations of your target country in detail, but normally there are strong similarities within the European Union.

FAMILY

The first option for the sponsor is if you have a partner who is a citizen of the country or works/studies there and can prove that they can maintain you.

If you have a partner in the EU country, they need to apply for a special visa, a provisional residence permit (mvv). This visa allows you to enter the country and is valid for 3 months. When you arrive in the country you need to make an appointment with the Immigration authorities and collect your residence permit.

Your partner will apply for the mvv visa and residence permit at the same time. They need to check whether they meet the conditions.

Conditions for your partner (EU citizen):

The government does not want you to make use of public funds, such as social benefits, to be able to live together with your partner. Therefore, your sponsor must have sufficient independent, long-term means of support.

Conditions for you

You need to pass the basic civic integration exams abroad. You should also not be a danger to public order and national security and do a TB (tuberculosis) test.

Conditions for both of you

You have a relationship together. This means: you are married, or you have a registered partnership, or you are not married but have a long-term and exclusive relationship with each other. You must live together in the destination country at the same address. You must also register with this address in the Personal Records Database in your municipality. To register, the municipality will ask for a translated and legalized birth certificate. Make sure you bring this certificate with you when you travel to your destination country.

Procedure

Collect the documents

In your application, you must show that you meet the conditions. You do this with documents. Collect the documents on your checklist before you submit the application. Start in good time, because it may take a while, for example, because you need to have documents from abroad. You often need to have foreign documents legalized and translated.

Fill out the form online

Have you collected all the documents? Then you can fill out the form. You can usually submit the application online on the website of the Immigration authorities.

Wait for a decision

You receive an acknowledgment of receipt of your application. This letter also states when you will receive an answer to your application. This is the decision period.

You receive the decision from the Immigration authorities

The Immigration authorities have decided on your application: it has either been approved or rejected.

Travel to the destination country

If the decision is positive, you can travel to the destination country. If your partner also applied for an mvv visa for you, then you first collect the mvv in the destination country's embassy or consulate in your home country.

STUDY

The process is similar; the only difference is that your university or business school acts as your "sponsor" and submits the application for you.

Submit the application

The application for an mvv visa is submitted by your university or business school.

The educational institution applies for the mvv and the residence permit at the same time, using the application form. The educational institution sends the application to the Immigration authorities. The Immigration authorities collect the fees for the application from your educational institution.

Receipt and check application

Your educational institution will get a confirmation letter once the application has been received. The confirmation letter states the date when it was received as well as the period within which the decision will be made.

Decision

The Immigration office checks whether you and your educational institution meet all the conditions required for the residence permit. If so, you will get an mvv and a residence permit.

You collect the mvv from the consulate or embassy in your home country. You have 3 months to collect it. Please make an appointment for this. Your passport must be valid for at least 6 months on the day you get the mvv. You have to provide your biometric information upon collection.

Travel to the destination country

Once you have collected your mvv, you can travel to the destination country. The mvv is valid for 90 days. The validity is shown on the mvv sticker.

After the application: Collect your residence permit

The Immigration office aims to have the residence permit ready within 2 weeks after the positive decision. They will send your educational institution a letter indicating when you can collect the residence permit. For this, you have to make an appointment online at the location stated in the letter.

Registration with the municipality

Upon arrival, you must normally register at the municipality where you are going to live. To register with the municipality you need a legalized and translated birth certificate, so take this when you travel to the destination country.

Take out health insurance

Please check if you are required to have basic health insurance and make sure you arrange it because it can be a legal requirement.

Validity residence permit

The residence permit for study is valid for the duration of your education plus 3 months. You can get 1 extra year for a preparatory education course or a transition year.

WORK

In this case the company you are going to work for acts as the sponsor of your visa.

The most common situations are highly skilled migrant or researcher (if you plan to do a Ph.D.).

Highly skilled migrant

You are going to work in a high-level position. Specific salary requirements apply. Your employer must be recognized as a sponsor by the Immigration office. For this residence permit, you cannot apply yourself. Your employer should apply for the residence permit.

European Blue Card

The European Blue Card is intended for employees who perform highly skilled work within the EU. Specific salary and educational requirements apply. This residence permit also makes it easier for the employee to work in a different EU Member State. You cannot apply for this permit yourself; your employer must apply.

Researcher within the meaning of Directive (EU) 2016/801

You can also work as a researcher within the meaning of Directive (EU) 2016/801. You do not need to receive a salary; you may also receive a grant. Your employer must be recognized as a sponsor. For this residence permit, you cannot apply yourself; your employer should apply.

Steps in the application process

Find a job in the EU

Usually, you can only obtain a residence permit for the purpose of work if you have an offer from your employer and they are willing to sponsor you.

Option A: You worked for the same company in your home country, and they are going to transfer you to another location within the EU.

Option B: you found a job in the EU from your home country, and after completing all the interviews they made an offer.

Personally, I know more people who followed the route Study => Search Year => Highly Skilled Migrant => Permanent residence => Citizenship. But it is also possible to get a job directly; you just need to have a very convincing story why they should hire and relocate you. It means that your perceived value should be high enough for them to make the extra effort.

Your employer applies for your residence permit

In order to travel to the EU, you need a temporary residence permit (mvv). The mvv is a sticker that the consulate / embassy places in your passport. Your employer applies for the temporary residence permit (mvv) and the combined permit for residence and work (gvva) at the same time.

Decision

The Immigration office checks whether you meet all conditions. If you and your employer meet all conditions, you will receive an mvv (if required) and a residence permit. The Immigration office will inform the employer of this decision.

Picking up your mvv and/or travel to the destination country

You can pick up the mvv at the consulate or embassy in your home country. You have 3 months to pick it up. Make an appointment for this. It can sometimes take a few weeks before you can collect your mvv from the consulate or embassy.

Picking up the residence permit

The Immigration office tries to have the residence permit ready within 2 weeks after the positive decision or after collecting your biometric data. You will receive a letter telling you when you can pick up the permit. You do not need to make an appointment to pick up your residence permit, but you can make one if you prefer.

Registration with the municipality

Upon arrival in the Netherlands, you must register in the municipality where you are going to live. To register with the municipality you need a legalized and translated birth certificate.

Take out health insurance

Normally if you work in the country you must take out health insurance. Please check the conditions for your country of destination.

Highly skilled migrant: conditions

There are certain conditions that apply to everyone. In addition, you and your employer have to meet the following conditions:

- You have an employment contract with an employer or research institution

- This employer is a recognized sponsor

- You are going to earn sufficient income. The agreed salary is in accordance with market conditions. Depending on your age there are income requirements because the government expects highly skilled migrants to have well-paid jobs and be fully able to maintain themselves.

Just as an example, for the Netherlands the current requirements are:

Highly skilled migrants aged 30 years old or older: € 4,752 gross per month

Highly skilled migrants younger than 30 years old: € 3,484 gross per month

Reduced salary criterion: € 2,497 gross per month

European Blue Card: € 5,567 gross per month

30% Ruling if hired from abroad

If you are hired from abroad, you might be eligible for a 30% ruling, which means that the first 30% of your salary is exempt from tax. As a result, you will receive a higher net amount. It is a huge benefit. But it only applies if you were hired from abroad. If you first studied in the country and then got a job, you are normally not eligible for this benefit.

The 30% ruling is only valid for the first 5 years (at least in the Netherlands). Then your full salary will be taxed.

Conditions including the following will apply to make use of the 30% facility with effect from 1 January 2012:

- You have an employment relationship.

- You are recruited from another country by your employer, or you are sent from another country to your employer. In the 2 years before your 1st working day in the country, you lived outside the country for more than 16 months, at a distance of more than 150 kilometers from the border.

- You have specific expertise that is not or is only barely available on the local employment market.

- You have a valid decision.

Please check the specific requirements and conditions for your country. This is only to make you aware that in some cases there are important tax benefits and to make sure that you take them into consideration.

As you can see, to get a residence permit you need to meet simple and clear criteria.

- If you have a partner with sufficient income, they can arrange it for you
- If you are going to study, you just need to be accepted on the program, negotiate a scholarship and acceptable payment terms (see later in this book), and then your university or business school will submit an application for you

- If your company is relocating you or if you were hired from abroad, your employer will arrange a residence card, and additionally you can benefit from the 30% ruling

You can also consider hedging your bets, by, for example, applying for highly ranked programs in different countries as well as for medium or low ranked programs or business schools just to get your foot in the door and minimize costs. At the end of the day, execution is key: sometimes it is ok just to get admitted to any program in the country, so you have a reason to move there and start looking for a job when you are already there, which makes it easier both for you and your future employer.

Diversify your stakes, trust the process and take it one step at a time. It is absolutely possible to move to the EU and start building your life here, no matter where you started your journey.

MBA APPLICATION

MBA stands for Master of Business Administration. Essentially it is a one- or two-year program which provides a high-level overview of how different functions work together to achieve business objectives (Finance, Supply Chain, Marketing, Strategy, etc.). It also aims to strengthen participants' profiles (hard skills & soft skills) and prepare them for the next step in their career. Normally the next step involves changing location, industry, or function.

There are two types of MBAs: Executive (part-time) and Full Time. And two types of Business Schools: those in the top 30 of the Financial Times ranking, and those below the top 30.

Top business schools have a very strong alumni base, a highly recognizable brand, a strict selection process, and good connections with certain industries/companies. So, it is relatively easy to get a good job after graduating from the top schools. If you want to study with the best and are willing to put in a lot of effort you should definitely apply to one of them.

But that was not my choice – for various reasons that I will explain below. 😊

The majority of the top 30 schools are in the U.S.: only 6 European schools made it to the top in 2020.

The top 30 business schools are:

Rank in 2020	Rank in 2019	School name	Country	Weighted salary ($)	Salary increase (%)
1	2	Harvard Business School	U.S.	210,110	110
2	4	University of Pennsylvania: Wharton	U.S.	211,543	107
3	1	Stanford Graduate School of Business	U.S.	222,625	117
4	3	Insead	France / Singapore	181,277	101
5	5	Ceibs	China	185,103	187
6	8	MIT: Sloan	U.S.	197,177	119
7	6	London Business School	U.K.	171,492	105
8	9	Columbia Business School	U.S.	202,238	115
9	19	HEC Paris	France	164,529	133
10	7	University of Chicago: Booth	U.S.	191,679	123
11	14	Northwestern University: Kellogg	U.S.	186,438	109
12	10	University of California at Berkeley: Haas	US..	193,630	110
13	12	Iese Business School	Spain	151,347	119
14	11	Yale School of Management	U.S.	178,829	128
15	17	National University of Singapore Business School	Singapore	167,070	148
16	15	Dartmouth College: Tuck	U.S.	177,819	112
16	19	Duke University: Fuqua	U.S.	174,070	123

PART III: HOW

Rank in 2020	Rank in 2019	School name	Country	Weighted salary ($)	Salary increase (%)
18	23	University of Virginia: Darden	U.S.	170,240	128
19	16	University of Cambridge: Judge	U.K.	162,662	95
19	18	HKUST Business School	China	157,025	113
21	13	University of Oxford: Saïd	U.K.	156,739	103
22	25	New York University: Stern	U.S.	166,392	122
23	27	Cornell University: Johnson	U.S.	166,035	123
24	21	Esade Business School	Spain	140,686	117
25	22	IMD Business School	Switzerland	156,421	67
25	26	UCLA Anderson School of Management	U.S.	166,720	111
27	33	Indian Institute of Management Bangalore	India	183,703	157
28	24	Indian School of Business	India	161,174	188
29	31	SDA Bocconi School of Management	Italy	140,404	120
30	28	University of Michigan: Ross	U.S.	164,336	115

However, business schools outside the first tier are a perfect first step to land in the country, get familiar with the environment, get a search year visa after graduating, and then look for a job. Some of these schools also offer great scholarships/discounts, which will make your total cost much lower.

Of course, participants of the program, the school's brand, and alumni network are weaker compared to the top 30. But the upside is that mid-tier schools have a less competitive selection process and are cheaper.

In short:

Getting admitted to an MBA program in a European country is a good option to land in the country, get familiar with the environment, understand the market, then get a search year visa and start looking for a job.

Benefits of a top-30 school

- High quality of students due to competitive selection process
- Highly recognizable brand
- Strong alumni network
- High chance of getting a job right after graduation

Downsides of a top-30 school

- Difficult to get admitted due to competitive selection process
- Higher costs (less likely to give scholarships, because the demand is high)
- Probably this can be mitigated via getting a loan and financing your studies – check if the school assists in this area

Benefits of a second-tier school

- Easier to get admitted
- Lower costs (more likely to give scholarships) – especially private schools
- First step to land in the country & start looking for a job

Downsides of a second-tier school

- Weaker alumni network
- Weaker school brand (can be good enough within the country where the school is located, but not outside)

- Quality of students is moderate (less to learn from your classmates)
- Weak connections with companies: job search mainly depends on your own efforts

HOW TO APPLY

See an example below. It can vary depending on the school; this example is just to give you an idea of how it could work.

Course outline
1 year, English, 50 hours per week, € 37,500 (exempt from VAT), Full-time

Admission requirements
- Bachelor's degree or equivalent from an accredited institution
- A solid GMAT score (average is 620)
- Minimum of 3 years relevant full-time work experience (average is 7 years)
- Strong command of written and spoken English (TOEFL of 90 or IELTS of 6.5 is required)

Basically, you need to send your resume in English, a copy of your bachelor's degree diploma (translated to English) as well as two tests: GMAT and TOEFL.
It is really easy.

TOEFL is an English test. There are certified institutions in your home country, where you can complete it. Just find some sample tests and get familiar with test structure and conditions. Remember, you need to pre-

pare for this specific exam, not just brush up your English. To prepare for the exam you need to know:
- Types of questions/sections (for example listening, speaking, writing, etc.)
- Time given to answer them (per section)
- Examples (templates) of good answers
- How the scores are calculated

So, for example, you should not write long sentences where you can make more mistakes if it is enough to write short sentences. Or you should not spend too much time on one question, and fail to complete the exam on time. You also do not need to study all possible grammar rules, if it is not necessary for this specific exam. You only need to get 90+ points for your test: this is your objective.

Studying English or any other language is a broad topic with many variables. Preparing for a specific exam with a defined structure and scoring is a much narrower task. Make sure you do what is needed: prepare for the exam.

GMAT is the **Graduate Management Admission Test**: a computerized adaptive test (CAT) intended to assess certain analytical, writing, quantitative, verbal, and reading skills in written English for use in admission to a graduate management program, such as an MBA program. It requires knowledge of certain specific grammar, algebra, geometry, and arithmetic.

It is a tough test. The maximum score is 800. Top schools expect you to score above 700, while mid-tier schools would accept something over 620, but the exact number depends on the school.

What can I say about GMAT?

- It is a great test, really smart and adaptive which digs at your brain, checks your ability to think logically, solve problems as well as how fast you can do it
- It is a combination of logic, math, geometry, and grammar
- Time is critical
- It is an adaptive test (will explain below)
- As usual, you need to prepare for the test, not just improve your algebra or grammar.

GMAT is something you need to prepare for. This means you should join some preparation courses, get training materials, and access sample tests. You need to get familiar with the test structure, timing, and types of questions, as well as methods of answering them, such as how to eliminate options and make a better guess in case you do not know the right answer.

You can also Google some prep materials: it helps.

It is an adaptive test, which means if you answered a difficult question, the next question will be even more difficult. The test calibrates questions based on your level. So in the end most of the participants will answer the same number of questions correctly, but those who answer more difficult ones will get more points.

In my view, the best GMAT strategy is:

- Google it, and find out about the structure, types of questions, and time per question.
- Spend 2-3 weeks preparing and then schedule the GMAT exam, to get familiar with how it works, get real-life experience and understand your weaknesses. You will get a score and understand your current level.

- Then join the prep courses (maybe 2 months of intensive courses) and address your weaknesses. Do a lot of sample exams with timing.
- Then do a 2nd test. Hopefully, your results will improve, and it will be enough to meet the school's requirements.
- A higher score normally strengthens your negotiation position with the school and makes you more attractive for them as a student. A lower score can be balanced with a stronger resume/profile or diverse experience that can contribute to the overall diversity of the group.

A high GMAT score does not guarantee admission, just as a low score doesn't preclude admission. Schools might accept students with lower GMAT scores if they believe this can be offset by stronger areas in the candidate's profile. While a solid GMAT score is important, it is not necessarily a deal-breaker.

Interview

Upon receipt of your application, the school will contact you to arrange an interview. Normally it can be done via Skype or in person if it is a possibility.

Basically, the interview is a one-hour call to discuss your profile, motivation, and so on. The focus is on how you can contribute to the group and profile of the school, and on your motivation (so they have confidence that you will proceed if they admit you).

Costs (example)

It depends on the country and rank of the school, but it will probably be something between € 30-50K. But you can get a scholarship which reduces this cost by 60-80%. And you can get a loan or negotiate a payment schedule for the reminder. Do not let high costs stop you!

The price normally includes:
- Application fee
- Enrollment fee (€ 2-10K, paid before you start studying). Sometimes it is all you have to pay.
- All study books
- All reading materials
- All study trips

Additional costs (not included in program price):
- Personal and medical insurance costs amount to around € 50-100 per person per month
- For an overseas student, living costs, including accommodation, insurance, and general expenses, amount to around € 1000 per month.

Scholarships

Business schools understand the financial commitment of funding an MBA. Many of them offer substantial merit scholarships to qualified candidates. Most scholarships are essay-based and all essays should reflect your point of view expressed in your own words. The quality of the admission application will also be taken into consideration.

How scholarship decisions are made

When making scholarship decisions, the admissions board reviews all application materials submitted by candidates and assesses each candidate's overall qualities: the academic profile, strength of overall admissions application, quality of admissions interview, and employability.

So basically, you need to make a good pitch and there is a good chance that you will qualify.

Loan Programs

There are loans to international students at the world's top business schools. The loan is available to candidates who have been accepted to the International Full-Time MBA program.

You need to proactively ask your school about loan programs they can suggest.

Tax Deduction

International Full-Time MBA fees and study-related expenses may be tax-deductible.

It means that when you finish your studies and get a job (so when you start paying tax), you can deduct these costs from your income and claim tax back. You can only claim tax back from the tax you've paid, so you cannot claim it immediately (while studying). But you can get the tax back when you start working and paying tax.

Visa help

Schools will assist you in all your visa application matters. Whether you need visa advice or want them to take care of the whole procedure, they have international offices dedicated to helping you with your visa concerns.

Residency Permit

Non-EU students must have a residency permit in addition to their visa.

The International Office will guide you through the process, or advise you further.

What the schools need from you

To successfully handle your visa and residency permit applications, schools normally need the following:

- a copy of your acceptance letter (provided by the school)
- a copy of all relevant passport pages
- proof of sufficient funding, either by you, by a sponsor, or jointly

Regarding "sufficient funding": you need to check with your school, but normally you need to show a certain amount of money in your account or the account of your sponsor (can be somebody from your family). It is a snapshot of your account, so you can consider temporarily borrowing money to arrange the bank statement.

It is important to note that a visa obtained through your business school is always restricted to a stay for study only.
Should you choose to remain in the country after graduation, you may be eligible to extend your stay and obtain a one-year residency extension for the purpose of finding work as a highly skilled migrant, or by starting an innovative company.

This scheme seeks to make settlement more attractive. It encourages exceptional foreign talents, of economic added value, to pursue career opportunities in the country where they studied. Once you have found suitable work (within a year), you can convert your one-year residency permit to that of a highly skilled migrant visa.

Housing

In many cases, schools will assist with a number of housing options.

They have agreements with rental agencies and offer fully furnished apartments within walking distance of campus.

As you can see, the process is very simple. You just need to do a couple of tests, submit your application with 4 documents, have a Skype call, get accepted, and then the school will help you with arranging the documents and even with finding accommodation. You can apply to multiple schools, so you have options in case you are rejected somewhere or if you want to have more flexibility with conditions and costs.

We will calculate living costs later. Just keep in mind that all costs are spread across multiple months. While it is ideal to have enough money for the whole year (including tuition fee and living costs), if you have some idea how to generate additional income or get additional funding after starting the program, just go for it, even if you have only 50% of what is needed. Also do not hesitate to negotiate a payment schedule and postpone payments as much as possible until you get a job and have a salary.

This brings us nicely to the next topic: "Negotiating your scholarship"

NEGOTIATING YOUR SCHOLARSHIP

Your tuition fee can be anything from € 0 to 100K. Also, your payment schedule can be anything from 100% pre-payment to starting paying 3 years after you graduate. Partially it depends on the practice of the specific school (which is NOT published on their website, hence you need to figure it out during your dialogue with them), and partially it depends on your negotiation skills.

There are two things you should know about negotiation:

It is important to understand the deal-breaking position of your counterparty. You can find this by making extreme moves/offers. Do not assume that you know the deal-breaking position. The signal that you have not reached it is if they answer "yes" or "maybe". You get closer to the deal-breaking point only when they start saying "no". This is where you really start your negotiation. You should always try to get the maximum of what they can give, not just something they are comfortable with.

#1 Your strength in negotiation depends on your ability to say "no" and walk away at any point. *You can achieve this by having multiple options.*

Let me illustrate these two points with examples.

#2 *It is important to understand the deal-breaking position of your counterparty*

During my MBA, we had a negotiation skills workshop, in which we did a very insightful exercise. Two students were assigned to two roles: supplier and purchaser. They were requested to maximize the output of the negotiation.

The supplier was given the target price of their material, and the purchaser was given the target price to purchase it. These prices were not shared with the other party.

If the supplier was able to sell their goods 1 euro above the target price, they won 1 euro. If the purchaser was able to buy 1 euro below the target price they also won 1 euro.

And here's what happened:

Group 1

The supplier started the discussion by asking the purchaser what price they are willing to pay. The purchaser gave a price 3 euros below their target price. The supplier gladly agreed to the price. The purchaser was happy, assuming they had won 3 euros and that that was a good result.

Group 2

The supplier offered the purchaser goods for a price 3 times higher than their target price. The purchaser offered 1 euro less. The supplier gladly agreed, feeling happy about the transaction.

After the exercise was finished, suppliers and purchasers were allowed to share their input prices with each other.

And then they realized, that:

All suppliers were given the price of 2 euros, while all purchasers were given the price of 90 euros.

The difference in input was huge.

So if the supplier was able to sell their goods for 8 euros (4 times their target price) they still missed 82 euros. If the purchaser was able to buy for 80 euros (10 euros under their target price) they still missed 78 euros of opportunity.

The professor explained that the right negotiation strategy is to ask questions instead of making offers, and if that doesn't help, to make extreme offers without disclosing your target price, and spend a lot of time calibrating the offer, until you get to the point where your counterparty starts saying no. For example, the purchaser should have started with 1 euro. When they got a no, they should have offered two euros. If this price was accepted by the supplier (for whom it was a target price and who had no idea that for the purchaser the target was 90) then it would have been a successful negotiation for the purchaser.

This is how you should negotiate your scholarship.

If you are a purchaser (a student), and the business school is a supplier, after receiving an acceptance letter (which means that the school considers you as their future student and already invested some time and money in recruiting you) you should start by saying that you have very little or no money and ask them if they can offer you a full discount.

Obviously, it is an extreme offer, but it is just a starting point of your negotiation. It also calibrates their expectations from you, so they will go for a minimum acceptable fee right away. If they say no, then you may ask what a maximum available scholarship is and how to get it.

If the scholarship they offer is insufficient, you can ask what you can do to increase it.

If the tuition fee is € 40K, do not assume that you must pay € 40K. Start from zero and work your way up to the absolute minimum they can accept. When you reach this minimum after several rounds of communication (let's say it is € 8-10K), then ask if there are institutions which can provide an educational loan for this amount. Sometimes they mention this on their website.

Once the amount and the way to finance it are settled, also make sure that you have the best possible payment schedule, which means you pay small installments and as late as possible – ideally after you get a job and start generating an income.

In short, the algorithm is:

- Start by building a high perceived value for yourself by communicating how you can contribute to the group with your experience as well as to the ranking of the school after you graduate. You can also say that you will be an ambassador of the school in your country and support them in recruiting more students
- Explain your financial difficulties and your aspiration to do an MBA at their school
- Ask about the maximum available scholarship
- After you get it – ask for more
- When they say no – this is their limit
- Stick to their absolute minimum amount and then ask if they have a partner who can provide a student loan (also do your own Goo-

gle search to see what the criteria are to apply, taking into account that you were admitted)
- Irrespective of whether you can get a loan or not, negotiate with the school about the payment schedule, aiming to postpone as much as possible to the time when you have a job and enough income to pay them back

Do not be shy to discuss difficulties with paying the tuition fee. You were already accepted to the school, so they see the value in inviting you. And there will always be a way to solve financial questions.

If your budget is very limited, Google schools that give more scholarships or scholarships that cover all costs before applying. In some cases, to get a scholarship you need to write an essay or something like this, and these 3-4 pages of text can save you up to € 30K.

#2 Your strength in negotiation depends on your ability to say no and walk away at any point.

If you can say no and walk away, you have a lot of power. You can achieve this by maximizing the number of options (up to the point where you can manage them).

Apply to many schools, so your stakes are distributed. Then you can compare their offers and conditions and decide what works best. If you are short of money, you can give up some advantages of highly ranked schools and go for mid- or low-tier but you will get to the country anyway.

And when you apply for a job after completing your MBA, the name of your school only matters if it is in top 30. Otherwise, it's not really relevant; your future employer will care much more about your experience and communication skills than about your educational background.

Most of my friends who completed an MBA managed to get 50-85% discounts on tuition fees. And then they negotiated a payment schedule (for example – to pay the remainder after they graduated and got a job) or applied for loans that could be paid later.

Do not take things at face value and do not stress too much about the finances.

Negotiate hard, and you can save a lot of money just with a couple of emails or phone calls. Maybe it won't be the most comfortable experience, but it is better to go through it in 1-2 days than to get stuck with an extra € 20-30K to pay to the school and get stressed over the next few years about where to get the money from.

So where can you actually get the money?

Ideally you get a long-term, low-interest loan in Europe (applies only for tuition).

If not, you can borrow from your family or use your savings, if you have them.

Consider how you can shift/regroup your assets to extract some extra money – rent your apartment, sell it and buy something smaller / in a different location, etc.

Think if there is a chance to get some part-time remote job in your home country to make a few hundred extra while studying and looking for a job. Maybe there are some government-funded programs or scholarships in your home country or something provided by the school.

It can be a combination of the options above.

In my case, I sold my apartment in the city center, and bought a similar one in a less expensive neighborhood, and then used the difference in price to pay the first installment (€ 4K) and living costs of the first 3-4 months.

I continued working remotely, and it helped to survive. I also negotiated to pay the rest of my tuition later and was paying it in small installments when I got a job. I also got an internship with a monthly salary of € 1.5K (after tax), which helped to pay rent for a few months. Maybe it was a bit bumpy sometimes, but I survived, and so will you.

Just do not get stressed about the money, get the total cost to a minimum, negotiate the best possible payment terms and combine multiple options to get the necessary amount. There were not so many rich people in my class, but each of them managed to get just enough to get there. And so will you.

CONFIRMATION AND PREPARING FOR THE MOVE

Congratulations: you have received the school acceptance letter or a job offer, mvv visa, booked your accommodation (at least for the first few months) and now you are ready to move.

What do you need to take care of before you fly?

Documents

- Legalized translation of your birth certificate with apostille (easy)
- Passport with mvv visa
- Health insurance (you will need local insurance, but you should also arrange something in your home country for the first few months, just in case, as it is not expensive and can be helpful)
- Admission letter

Medical stuff

- Do a check-up and fix whatever needs to be fixed
- Visit your dentist: in Europe it is expensive and is not covered by insurance
- Buy all necessary medications, especially if they are easy to buy and do not require prescriptions. In Europe you need a prescription for everything; only paracetamol is widely available and is used as a cure for all medical conditions

What to take with you?

- Good laptop & phone: these are your main instruments of communication
- A couple of books you can dive into in the evening if you are overwhelmed with your new life
- Some nice movies on your hard drive or on your device to get distracted
- Sports shoes & clothes: if you experience stress there is nothing better than exercise
- Your favorite spices or stuff you won't be able to buy easily and need for cooking

In the end, you will only have a couple of suitcases, right? So if you have documents and money you should be fine. You can't take enough for the whole year, so keep it simple.

The main thing about moving abroad and all the overwhelming anxiety it can bring is: take it step by step.

Do not think about how you will survive the whole year; think about how to order a taxi to the airport.

Then think about what to eat or watch when on the plane.

Then what train to take to get to your accommodation.

Then what to cook for dinner.

Then just get a bottle of wine or beer, open it, and have a drink.

Watch a movie or read a book, sleep and wake up late.

PART III: HOW

Take a shower, get dressed, walk around the neighborhood, and visit the supermarket.

Meet a couple of classmates (make a Facebook or WhatsApp group).

Visit the school. Find a sports center or a swimming pool. Join some sports lessons (yoga, badminton, soccer on the weekend, etc.)

When the classes start and you meet your classmates, you will get drawn into daily activities and there will be no time to worry. Make sure you solve the problems as they arise. Do not try to sort out lifelong issues within a day. Do not look too often at the horizon, at least in the beginning. Take it step by step.

And when you make a hundred small steps, you will get to your old horizon, and see a new one far away. Live in the present, deal with the task at hand and complete it to the best of your ability.

Get inspired by your own bravery.

Maybe only 0.1% of the population of your home country dared to travel abroad, settle there, redefine themselves and choose their own path. Because it is so much easier to stay where you are (and so uninspiring). Just think about your city, your country, your neighborhood – how many of your neighbors took off to Europe?

Very few.

But you did.

And now you are not reading about somebody else's journey any more, but you are the hero of the story which is unfolding in front of you. Make it a nice one – full of laughter, bravery, insights, and inspiration. Live your life like you're the hero in the movie.

And if you are in doubt, or need support, try to find like-minded people around you to share your worries and aspirations. Fly with eagles. Or otherwise just drop me a line!

PART IV:
FIRST YEAR

REGISTERING AT THE MUNICIPALITY, RESIDENCE CARD, BANK ACCOUNT, GP, INSURANCE

There are several things you need to do in the first few months.

Register at the municipality & get a citizen service number (BSN)

Maybe it depends on the country, but in the Netherlands, you need to register at the municipality so they know where you live and can send you all kinds of communication from the government. You also need to get your unique number (in NL we call it BSN). This number will be used as your unique identifier across different government-run institutions and platforms. The government uses your citizen service number (BSN) to process your personal data. You can use your BSN for any government service in the Netherlands. You do not have to provide your data to each different government organization – they can find it using your BSN.

Convert your mvv visa to a residence card (study, work, or partnership)

Your sponsor (university, business school, employer, or your partner) should be informed of the date when your residence card is available for pick-up. Then you can schedule an appointment with the Immigration authorities and pick it up.

Open a bank account

It is good to have a local bank account. You can check if your sponsor (for example business school) already has some agreements or recommendations. Otherwise, you can check with one of the main banks in the country about the conditions for opening a bank account. Normally if you are a resident and have a citizen number you should be able to open an account. Then you can transfer the money from the account of your home country or deposit cash.

Register with GP (general practitioner, doctor)

The health system can be slightly different depending on the country. For the Netherlands it works like this:

- You need to find a doctor near to your home and register with them. This means you need to call them or send an email, and then make an appointment to get introduced. Just Google based on your address or postcode.
- GP is included in the insurance (at least in NL)
- If you have a problem, call and make an appointment.
- In 99% of situations they prescribe paracetamol and send you home. So if you want to get something else, make the situation look dramatic when you visit them – do not hesitate to exaggerate.
- European health system heavily depends on two prescriptions: "Go home and do nothing. If it gets worse in two weeks, come again" and "Take paracetamol".
- To get an appointment with a specialist, you need to get a reference from your GP. Prepare your arguments in advance; they do not like sending you to a specialist, and would rather just ask you

to do nothing or take paracetamol and wait a couple of weeks. Anyway, just register with a GP – it is not like you have a lot of options
- If you are paranoid – go to Germany occasionally to do a full check-up (paid) and find a psychotherapist in your city to talk over your fears and worries.
- The European medical system can be shocking at times. Just try to understand it. It is very good for treating difficult cases – great hospitals, modern equipment, everything is paid for by insurance. So if you are in trouble, they will make you better, though there might be some waiting time. And it has very low sensitivity to everything else (medium / low disturbance cases and all kinds of prevention). Unless your legs are dropping off or you lost 4 liters of blood they do not think you have any health problems.

Health insurance

a. You need to have Basic Health Insurance. You pay between 80-120 euros per month if you have income. If you do not have any income, you can apply for an allowance and receive approx. 75 euros per month from the government. You can choose your own risk: from approx. 400 to 800 euros. If you pay the lowest premium, you take the highest own risk (approx. 800 euros). It means that you have to pay the first 800 euros of any medical expenses (within a year) yourself. EVERYTHING above this amount (surgery, hospital costs, etc.) will be paid for by insurance. So basically if you pay around 80 euros per month, you have a fixed cost of 960 euros per year, plus 800 euros of your own risk. Everything else (no matter what it is) will be paid for by insurance. Basically, it means that you should be able to fix all minor issues yourself,

and you are fully covered for any major issues. This cost includes prescribed medications.
b. All insurance companies offer more or less the same conditions. Look for a) a relatively big company/brand, so they have some scale and are not super-niche, b) good customer support, and c) good online portal (all of them try to minimize costs and reduce interactions with you, so at least their online portal should be ok). There are websites to compare insurance companies/packages, so check them out.
c. Dental care is not included. In NL, the average bill is 60-250 euros, depending on the complexity of your problem.
d. A GP (General Practitioner) visit is included in insurance, so there is no cost for visiting the doctor.

These are basic steps you need to take to have your documents in order and start building your "infrastructure".

You should consider some of the following:

- **Find an internet provider.** Normally they have combined packages – TV & Internet. There is no life without the internet. Then you can also subscribe to all kinds of streaming platforms like Netflix.
- **Get a local SIM card**
- **If there is a Digital ID in your country, register and get it.** Then you should be able to do many operations online, like registering at a new address, and requesting all kinds of services from the municipality or the government.
- **Get a personalized transport card & check what kind of subscriptions are available.** Normally you can use this card for all transport, and it allows you to save money by only paying for

the distance you traveled. It also gives you discounts in off-peak hours
- **Get discount/loyalty/bonus cards from local supermarkets**
- **Find a gym, a swimming pool, or join any kind of sports club** (badminton, tennis, yoga). Ideally, it should be a group sport, so you can also start building your social circle
- **Join Facebook groups like Expats in (name of the country / your city)** – you can ask your questions there or just get some tips from other members of the group
- **Figure out where & when there is a local open market** where you can buy all kinds of food they do not sell in the supermarket
- **Find the closest park** so you can walk/run there when the weather is nice
- **Find an Asian shop, wine shop, and register at the pharmacy**
- **Say hello to your neighbors**, so you feel that you live in the community and not on your own
- If you plan to stay long-term, **start learning the language.** In most European countries there are government-subsidized courses. In the Netherlands, there is https://www.nltraining.nl/ where you pay 40 euros for 6 months of lessons.

ACCOMMODATION

Finding accommodation can be challenging.

But it also depends on the reason why you are moving to the EU.

If it is a partnership residence card, then you can (and sometimes must) stay with your partner.

If it is a highly skilled migrant visa – check with your employer, maybe they provide temporary accommodation, so you have more time to look around and arrange viewings when you arrive in your destination country.

If it is a study / MBA residence card – it is also possible that your university or business school has some options available for their students. This is how it worked in my case. The business school offered studios/apartments to their students, at reasonable prices and located near the university.

The first piece of advice is: ask your sponsor (partner, employer, or university) if they offer accommodation. It is really much better than trying to find something yourself, so push them as hard as you can.

If they do not offer accommodation, it gets tricky.

Normally if it is a popular location, there will be more people wanting to rent than the number of apartments available. The landlord has more bargaining power and will go for the safest and most reliable choice, i.e., somebody local (from the same country or from the EU) and with sufficient income to pay the rent. They can also ask for evidence of your funds, which is difficult to provide if you have not arrived to the country yet.

My suggestion would be:

- Use local internet resources (websites that can help find a place in a specific country)
- Consider temporary accommodation so you can stay there for a while and have more flexibility when looking for something long-term
- It is ok to rent a room for a short time if you cannot find a proper independent place
- Connect to alumni in the country or join Facebook groups "Expats in XXX (your destination country)" and ask for advice or ask them to share their experiences
- While you are alive, everything is possible, so maintain a "zero doubt" attitude – sooner or later you will find a solution

Depending on your country/purpose of stay you might be eligible for a housing allowance. This is an allowance from the government if you do not have enough income to pay for your accommodation. I believe this allowance is mainly to cover your rental costs (i.e., not utilities). If you are eligible, please apply for it. For example, if you are a student with a valid residence permit and you do not have any income at the moment, then in some countries you can apply for a housing allowance that will cover part of your rent. Google or check the website of Tax authorities to see if you are eligible.

The last thing you need to know about rent is: it is the worst way to pay for your accommodation. Because if you pay rent, you are simply opening the window once a month and throwing the money away.

It is better to get a mortgage and buy a place – but of course, you can only do that once you have a stable long-term income.

Why is renting so bad?

Let's say in the Netherlands you need € 1.2K per month for a one-bedroom apartment. But you will pay more or less the same monthly installment (mortgage) for a 100 sq. m. apartment/house.

Around 200 euros will be paid back by tax authorities (interest is tax-deductible).

So in the case of rent, you lose € 14.6K annually with a 50 sq. m. apartment

If you pay € 14.6K annually as a mortgage you:
- Get € 2.4K back from the tax office
- Have a 100 sq. m. place
- Part of your € 14.6K payment is a down payment, so it is actually your asset and you can get it back when you sell the house
- Your house can increase in value, so you can (potentially) get more when you sell it later
- Nobody can kick you out (while you pay your mortgage)
- Interest rates can be very low, so you lose very little, even in the long term
- There are insurance programs to protect you from the situation

when house price drops below purchase price (which is not very likely)
- You feel more settled because you own the property, and do not feel like a guest anymore

To summarize, the most important things you need to know about the accommodation in the EU are:

Put as much pressure as possible on your sponsor to help you with accommodation

If it is not possible, accept something temporary first and then look for a better option

Buy a house as soon as possible to reduce financial waste

Build your assets and sell when the market is high, then move somewhere else, because the world has around 200 countries and you are not obliged to live in only one or two

The world is flexible if you can flex it

LIVING COSTS

I live in the Netherlands, so my calculation is based on the prices in this country.

All numbers are from 2021.

Let's look at 3 options:

- Low-profile student
- Student / employee with savings or comfortable salary
- All-out hedonist who really enjoys life.

Living costs have several important components:

- Rent or mortgage
- Transportation
- Insurance
- Food
- Sport/memberships
- Everything else

Low-profile student

Rent

You can rent a room in a shared apartment for 300-400 euros (depending on the city). If you are a student, nice, subsidized studios might be provided by the university/business school.

In some cases you can claim housing allowance – please check the information on the website of the tax office.

Utilities

Normally they are included in the rent if it is a shared apartment.

Health insurance

In the Netherlands, minimal health insurance is around 80 euros. You can claim a health insurance allowance in some cases.

Transportation

The best way to pay for public transportation is to get a chip card, so you only pay for the distance you traveled, which is normally less than a full-price ticket. There are also various subscriptions for the owners of such cards (off-peak travel, weekend travel, fixed price for a fixed route, etc.). If we assume that you use public transportation moderately, it could be around 60 euros per month.

Obviously, if your house is near the university/office, then your costs are lower. Or you can get a secondhand bike and cycle around.

Food

There are more expensive shops as well as discounters like Lidl. But if you want to eat properly, you need something between 50-70 euros per week, hence around 300 euros per month. It is always possible to just eat rice, but it is not very healthy.

Subscriptions

Internet + TV subscription is around 50 euros per month

Netflix: 15 euros.

Cell phone: let's say another 30 euros.

Fitness center, sport, supplements

On average you have to pay around 20-30 euros per month for a fitness center or swimming pool membership. It is cheaper if it is from the university. It is worth paying for: sport is very important, especially in high-stress situations.

Clothes

Pair of shoes: 60-100 euros
Shirt: 20-30 euros
Pants: 40-70 euros
Let's say if you buy one item of clothing every 2 months, you need something like 80 euros per month.

Total:

Rent: € 350
Health insurance: € 75
Transportation: € 60
Food: € 300
Subscriptions (internet, TV, cell phone): € 80
Fitness center: € 25
Clothes: € 80
TOTAL: € 970

So your minimum monthly bill is around 1,000 euros

An employee with savings or comfortable salary

Rent

You can rent a studio for 500-1000 euros, depending on the city. If you are a student, nice, subsidized studios might be provided by the university/business school.

In some cases you can claim housing allowance – please check the information on the website of the tax office.

Utilities

Normally they are included in the rent if it is a shared apartment. If not, heating, gas & electricity is around 90 euros, and water is around 15 euros per month.

Health insurance

In the Netherlands, minimal health insurance is around 80 euros. You can claim a health insurance allowance in some cases.

Transportation

The best way to pay for public transportation is to get a chip card, so you only pay for the distance you traveled, which is normally less than a full-price ticket. There are also various subscriptions for the owners of such cards (off-peak travel, weekend travel, fixed price for a fixed route, etc.). If we assume that you use public transportation more extensively, it could be around 100 euros per month.

Obviously, if your house is near the university/office, then your costs are lower. Or you can get a secondhand bike and cycle around.

Food

There are more expensive shops as well as discounters like Lidl. If you would like to get some nice fish, meat or cheese, as well as a bottle of wine from time to time, your weekly check is around 100 euros.

Subscriptions

Internet + TV subscription is around 50 euros per month
Netflix: 15 euros.
Cell phone: let's say another 30 euros.

Fitness, sport, supplements

On average you have to pay around 20-30 euros per month for a fitness center or a swimming pool. Let's say you also want to join yoga classes and visit the spa once a month. I would say plan something around 60 euros per month. It is cheaper if it is from the university. It is worth paying for: sport is very important, especially in high-stress situations.

Clothes

Pair of shoes: 60-100 euros
Shirt: 20-30 euros
Pants: 40-70 euros
Let's say if you buy one piece of cloth every month, then put something like 120 euro per month.

Total:

Rent: € 800 (studio)
Health insurance: € 80
Transportation: € 100
Food: € 400
Subscriptions (internet, TV, cell phone): € 80
Fitness: € 60
Clothes: € 120
TOTAL: € 1640

The main contributor to the increased bill is rent. The upside is that you will have your individual place, even though it could be a small studio.

An all-out hedonist who really enjoys life

Rent

You can rent an apartment with two bedrooms for € 1500-2000K. In this case, it is unlikely that you can claim the allowance since the cost of this apartment is above the basic level. If you have a partner this cost can be shared.

Utilities

Normally they are included in rent. If not, assume approx. 120 euros on utilities.

Health insurance

In the Netherlands, minimal health insurance is around 80 euros per month. Let's say you want to include a couple of visits to the dentist; then you end up somewhere around 150 euros per month.

Transportation

The best way to pay for public transportation is to get a chip card, so you only pay for the distance you traveled, which is normally less than a full-price ticket. There are also various subscriptions for the owners of such cards (off-peak travel, weekend travel, fixed price for a fixed route, etc.). A card with all included costs is around 360 per month, but is probably not necessary: you can get a really nice subscription for 150 euros per month.

Obviously, if your house is near the university/office, then your costs are lower. Or you can get a secondhand bike and cycle around.

Food

Meat, fish, wine, and vegetables should not cost more than 500 euros per month per person. This should be more than enough.

Subscriptions

Internet + TV subscription is around 50 euros per month
Netflix: 15 euros.
Cell phone: let's say another 30 euros.

Fitness center, sport, supplements

Swimming pool, sauna, gym & yoga – I do not see how it can be more than 100 euros per month.

Clothes

Pair of shoes: 60-100 euros
Shirt: 20-30 euros
Pants: 40-70 euros
Let's say if you buy one piece of clothing every month, then you will spend something like 120 euros per month.

Total:

Rent: € 1700
Health insurance: € 150
Transportation: € 150
Food: € 500
Subscriptions (internet, TV, cell phone): € 80
Fitness: € 100
Clothes: € 120
TOTAL: € 2650

So 2650-3000 euros should be enough to cover all your basic needs, excluding travel, buying expensive items such as a car, furniture, electronics, visiting restaurants/opera/concerts, etc.

Summary: you can spend anything between 900 and 3000 euros per month on your basic needs. You can also apply for some allowances to reduce this amount. Rent is the key contributor, so you need to choose between a room in a shared apartment, a studio, or a 1-2 bedroom apartment in the city center.

There might be even cheaper options provided by the university.

You might also be allowed to work a limited number of hours or work remotely to recover some of the costs. Anything above € 3K depends on your preferences and lifestyle. Of course, in some countries like Switzerland, prices can be much higher, while in others like Poland they can be much lower. This is just to give you an idea about the prices in a rather expensive country as well as about some main contributors to the total and some ways to reduce the cost.

ALLOWANCES

In some European countries, you can receive an allowance (payment) from the government to recover some unavoidable costs in case your income does not allow you to pay them.

This includes:

- Health insurance allowance
- Rent allowance
- Children allowance
- Tax back on your tuition fee
- Tax back on your mortgage interest rate

Let's review them in detail.

Health insurance allowance

If you do not have any income and still have to pay your health insurance, some countries might compensate you for this via monthly payments to your bank account. You need to check the conditions and the process on the website of the tax office of your country of residence.

Rent allowance

If you do not have enough income to pay your rent, in some countries you may be eligible for an allowance to contribute towards your rent.

Children allowance

In some countries, daycare is very expensive. You might be eligible for this allowance too.

Tax back on your tuition fee

Educational costs might be deductible from your income. It means when you start paying tax (from your salary, for example), you deduct your educational costs from your income, and the tax office will pay some of the tax you previously paid back, because your updated income is lower and hence you paid more tax than you should have paid.

For example: Your income in 2021 was € 70K, and you paid € 25K tax (based on the assumption that your income was € 70K). But if you deduct your tuition, for example € 20K, then your updated income is € 50K, and you should have paid less tax. So the tax office will pay part of your tax back.

Tax back on the interest rate of your mortgage

The interest rate of the mortgage (as well as a transfer tax) can be tax-deductible. This means you can deduct it from your income (one-off deduction for the transfer tax and yearly deduction for the interest rate) and get some money back.

In general, you should keep in mind the following:

- Tax in Europe is very high, so it is important to understand it well and use legal ways to minimize it where possible
- Consider hiring a tax advisor if relevant. If you pay substantial tax and have some items that can be deducted, the cost of hiring a tax advisor will normally be easily compensated by the tax you get back
- Usually, tax is filed on an annual basis
- Allowances can be paid monthly: for some of them you can easily apply yourself via the tax authority's website
- Investigate all allowances and tax-related topics to see if some of them are applicable in your case

MBA

An MBA is a one- or two-year program that gives you an overview of various functions of business (Accounting, Marketing, Strategy, Supply Chain, Micro/Macro economics, Statistics, Leadership, etc.) and prepares you for the next step in your career.

The result of getting an MBA is supposed to be:

- Next step in your career (leadership role)
- Change of industry, function or location

The key indicator of a successful MBA program is its place in the Financial Times ranking. 60% of this ranking is defined by the salary increase after getting an MBA.

Good MBAs have a strong brand and extensive alumni network.

To put it simply, there are two different games:

Real MBAs, where it is very difficult to get in and as a result, the quality of the group is extremely high. Therefore, companies are looking for the participants of these MBAs, and alumni are normally very successful people, just because of their incredible skills and talents. Still, it is possible to get into this group if you have a very high GMAT and contribute to the diversity of the group (have unique skills or experience that will complement the group).

Rest of the MBAs. Some of them can be strong brands in their home countries but unknown outside and some of them are not known at all. Here the quality of the group is not so great, so there is not much you can learn from your peers. But they might offer good discounts, be easy to get in to and be a good first step to get into the country.

If you have money, talent, and high ambition: try to get to first-tier MBAs.

If you are more on the lazy side and are looking to move to the EU with the minimum amount of effort, and also have a limited budget: try second-tier MBAs.

Apart from the brand value and quality of the group, an MBA is not about education, but people and experience. You will forget the content of most of the lectures, but you will learn how to live in a new country, how to interact with different kinds of people, and you will also buy yourself some time to understand the country you moved to and figure out whether you want to stay there.

This year will be one of the best years of your life.

- You will make new friends from many countries. Later you will visit these countries not as a stranger, but as a friend.
- You won't need to worry about your job, your boss, and all the stuff related to being an employee. It is like being back at school again, but this time you can drink, smoke, have sex, and enjoy sophisticated intellectual conversations.

- For the first 8 months you should simply relax and live in the moment. Focus on people and human interactions as much as you can.
- After 8 months you can start thinking about jobs, and trying to figure out what the job market looks like and what the criteria are to get a job. The best approach is to ask people from the previous groups who were the same as you now and somehow got jobs. Their experience will be the most relevant to you:
- What kind of companies did they join?
- What worked and what didn't?
- What contributed the most to their success?
- Do not overestimate your MBA degree: employers care much more about your experience than about your academic achievements; they do not care about the lectures you took or the theme of your thesis. An MBA is just a conversation opener, not a deal-breaker.

My suggestions regarding an MBA:

- Decide between a 1st and 2nd tier and act accordingly
- If it is a second-tier: minimize your costs, enjoy the first 8 months and focus on people
- Then connect to alumni who managed to get a job in your target country after graduating and ask what worked for them
- Do not overestimate the impact of the MBA: it is just an opportunity to land in the country and look around. Employers care about your experience and communication skills much more than they care about your degree
- Enjoy it, as it is going to be one of the best years of your life – you will be back to school, but this time you can drink, smoke, have sex, fall in love, and you are a deeper and more accepting version

of your old self. This is the period when you can take a vacation from your adult life while staying an adult on paper – what could be better than this?

Do ok academically, but do not over study – it does not impact the result. A good communicator is always much better than a nerd. People skills, communication skills & math make good leaders, not a perfect ten in every subject.

TRAVELING IN EUROPE

The beauty of Europe is that it is relatively small and very diverse at the same time. You can fly almost anywhere within 2-3 hours. And countries like Sweden, Switzerland, and Portugal are very different from each other, in terms of culture, food, landscape, climate, and architecture. So please, please travel a lot.

Normally, if you have a temporary residence permit, you do not need a visa, and there is no border control within the EU. You just need to check in your luggage, get your hand luggage checked and you are good to go.

There are plenty of low-cost airlines. Also, it is normally cheaper to take a connecting flight than a direct flight. You can use services like skyscanner.com to explore the options.

Try to travel at least once a month.

The rule of thumb is that countries in the south are cheaper than countries in the north. And people in small countries are more likely to speak English.

Here's a very brief overview:

My main criteria to score a country are:

- People and culture: vibe, energy, openness to communicate
- Landscape/scenery/nature: mountains, lakes, sea or ocean, food for the eye
- Food and wine: quality of local cuisine, and quality of wine or beer
- Architecture: what it feels like to walk on the streets of the city
- Prices: high or low

Austria: 7.5/10
Improved version of Germany. Classical music, nice white wines, the beautiful city of Vienna (stay inside the ring), not too expensive.

Belgium: 5/10
Brussels and Belgium in general are a bit messy. Very nice strong beer and nice food (influence of France). North is rich (Flanders) with some nice cities like Bruges (not very lively), Ghent (livelier), Antwerp. Brussels is nice in its own way, but in general, is a real mess.

Bulgaria: haven't visited.
The poorest country in the EU. Must be relatively cheap.

Croatia: 6/10
Some nice small cities on the coast (Rovinj, for example). Do not drink local wine.

Republic of Cyprus: haven't visited.

Czech Republic: 7/10
Prague is beautiful and relatively cheap. Good beer, different from German and Belgian. Definitely worth visiting, a good option for a budget trip.

Denmark: 8/10
The beautiful city of Copenhagen, very expensive, but still worth visiting. Consider visiting Christiania, if you like to see something new and unexpected, otherwise stick to the city center & Newhaven area.

Estonia: haven't visited

Finland: 7/10
Underrated and actually nice city of Helsinki. Even more expensive than Denmark though.

France: 8/10
Good wine (but use Vivino app and be selective, as there are also plenty of cheap and very bad wines), great museums. Paris is rather crowded and dirty, but you still can see a layer of history and beauty under the dust. Gets better in the evening, when things are not that much into your face. Don't forget the South of France and the villages.

Germany: 5/10
Berlin is great and very diverse, Hamburg is a bit nobler and better maintained, but apart from that Germany is kind of average. Haven't been to Bavaria yet. The rest is not to my liking.

Greece: 7/10
Beautiful islands, nice food, warm people, and great diversity of land-

scape. But Greece is not just one thing – it has hundreds of islands, so there is a lot to explore.

Hungary: 6/10
Nice view of the Parliament building from the opposite side of the river in Budapest, but in general Prague is better.

Ireland: 6/10

Italy: 7/10
You need to like it: good food, good wine, but I prefer a slightly different vibe.

Iceland: 8.5/10
Stunning!

Latvia: haven't visited

Lithuania: 6/10
Actually, quite nice, 2nd tier of European countries, if not the 3rd, but has its own vibe.

Luxembourg: haven't visited

Malta: haven't visited

Netherlands: 7.5/10
I live here at the moment. Beautiful cities, plenty of bikes and canals, egalitarian society. Definitely worth visiting. A bit flat – the landscape is always the same. People are rather reserved, not easy to make friends. At the same time, everyone speaks English.

Norway: 6.5/10
Beautiful nature, nice country, but not as impressive as, for example, Sweden.

Poland: haven't visited – just stopped at the airport.

Portugal: 9/10
Great food, amazing architecture, plenty of landscape, warm Mediterranean culture, Port wine and Madeira! I visited Lisbon (one of the most amazing cities), Porto, and Madeira. It is also relatively cheap there. If you can visit only one country in the EU, please go to Portugal.

Romania: haven't visited

Slovakia: haven't visited

Slovenia: haven't visited

Spain: 9/10
Spain is slightly below Portugal on my list, but it has more or less the same: great food, great wine, great people, plenty of sea & mountains, excellent architecture. Must visit!

Sweden: 8.5/10
Stockholm is an amazingly diverse and interesting city. Food is average, no local drinks, culture is kind of cold. I would rank it slightly higher than Copenhagen though due to its diverse landscape. Visit BodyFlight Stockholm!

Switzerland: 8.5/10
Damn expensive, local food is just ok, people are just ok but the scenery is fantastic!!!

My personal top 5:

1. **Portugal:** the best combination of food, culture, architecture, reasonable prices, and landscape.
2. **Spain:** almost the same as Portugal but very different ☺
3. **Switzerland or Iceland:** landscapes are amazing, prices are also amazing ☺
4. **France:** Paris is a city of contrasts, and Paris is not all France. But it is a very important cultural capital of the world (even if I only mention Impressionists) where every brick tells a story
5. **Sweden:** If you want to try something different – this is the #1 destination in Scandinavia.

SEARCH YEAR VISA

If your reason to travel to and stay in the country was a student visa, you are not allowed to work (or only allowed to work a very limited amount of time per week).

After graduating, you can apply for a search year visa. For this visa, you do not need a sponsor. This visa allows you to work (without the company being your sponsor), and unlike a highly skilled migrant visa, it doesn't have any salary requirements. Basically, it gives you time to find a job while legally staying in the country after you completed your studies.

If you have this visa, it means you can:

1. Work part-time legally
2. Extend your internship without your company needing to apply for a highly skilled migrant visa
3. You can also start a normal job or a temporary job, without requesting a highly skilled migrant visa from your employer
4. If you haven't found a job yet, you can stay in the country for one year (and also travel within the EU)

This visa is only valid for one year, so after that, your only option is to have a sponsor (a company or a partner) who can apply for your residence card.

Apply for a search year permit as late as possible, but still on time – when your student visa is about to expire or if you already received your diploma and graduated (in this case your business school or university will inform the Immigration office about your graduation, and you will receive a letter from them, because normally you can only legally stay in the country for 3 months after your graduation unless you apply for a search year visa).

I believe that the date when you apply will be the date of your search year visa, so if you applied while still having legal reasons to stay in the country you should be fine.

A search year visa is great. In my case I got a temporary job and was working with this visa, then I extended my contract to a one-year contract (while still on this visa), and then my employer applied for my highly skilled migrant visa. So it helped me to get to the company without having a dialogue about my visa, and then, when they already liked me and got used to me, it was much easier to convince them to apply for a highly skilled migrant visa.

To summarize: a search year visa is great, be aware that it exists, count on it in your plan, apply for it as late as you can and stay on it while looking for a job.

USEFUL TIPS FOR A NEWBIE

By now you already know a lot.

My main tips for the first chapter of your stay in the new country are:

If you do an MBA or educational program: do not think about a job for the first half of it and just enjoy your new life. You will never have this experience again.

Connect with people: this is the most important part of any success. All success in life comes through people, so be empathetic and improve your communication skills.

When things get difficult, focus on your actions and things you can control. Do not think about the things outside your control – it won't help.

If you don't know what to do, and feel stressed, worried or lost – go to the gym or swimming pool and exercise. Join group sports. Sweat. Get tired. Eat well. Then sleep. Your mind will feel much clearer after exercise, food, vitamins, sleep, and (if available) sex.

Read smart and difficult books because your brain is a muscle, and it also needs exercise.

Put things into perspective: there are 70 billion years before you were born, and another 70 billion years until this world disappears. Our feelings, worries, and situations are invisible in the fabric of time & space. Do not take yourself and your situation too seriously.

Remember: hard choices = easy life, easy choices = hard life. Make hard choices today to have an easy and beautiful life tomorrow.

Many people were in the same situation, and many will be. You are not alone.

Drop me a line!

PART V:
GETTING A JOB

WHERE TO LOOK FOR A JOB AND HOW TO SUCCEED

It is important to remember that a job is only one of the ways to generate income.

And sometimes it is not optimal for two reasons:

1. You exchange an irreplaceable and most valuable resource (time) for a replaceable and less valuable resource (money). This exchange directly ties your input (hours) to your output (salary) without any leverage / multiplicator to generate a better outcome.

Time is the most valuable asset you have. It is more important than money.

Any 90-year-old billionaire will gladly exchange all their wealth to be young again and have more time.

Having a job is selling your time for a fixed fee. Be mindful when selling your time – you do not have a lot of it, and you cannot recover lost time.

Also, you're not going to get rich renting out your time. You must own equity – a piece of a business – to gain your financial freedom. Fortunes require leverage. "Business leverage comes from capital, people, and products with no marginal cost of replication (code and media)".

You might need a job as a legal reason to stay in the country and cover your living costs. If you like what you do and it makes you happy, you can build a nice career. If you want to get rich instead, at a certain point you should seek financial freedom and use leverage (product, people, or capital) to generate wealth.

2. *Job as a low-risk activity leads to low reward.*

High risk = high reward. Low risk = low reward.

Having a job makes your situation relatively stable, but the low risk comes with low reward. If you want to climb above the average, you need to seek at least mid-risk situations.

But anyway, to get a highly skilled migrant visa you need a job.

And to get a job you need the following:

#1: INTENTION

For an expat, there is one key criterion that defines whether you will get a job or not: a clear intention to stay in the country. Everyone I know who really wanted to stay got a job. Everyone who had a plan B to go to their home country at the end of their visa flew back. To get a job in a new country is not an easy task, and only if you have a strong intention to stay you will get through all the hell and rejections and get to the other side.

#2: LUCK

A job search in developed countries with a high amount of competition very much depends on luck (unless you have connections and somebody can introduce you). Your immediate task is to get onto the candidate shortlist, but you really do not know – maybe they already have an internal candidate, maybe one of the selection criteria is more important than the rest (industry experience, etc.), and you won't know until they invite you to an interview. So you do not have a perfect set of data and cannot immediately get a job just by doing the right thing.

The best you can do is maximize the number of options, and the way to deal with luck is to flip the coin many times until it finally works.

#3: PERSISTENCE

The application process should be automated in order not to get involved emotionally.

1. Do research with keywords for your function and similar functions on LinkedIn to see where the numbers of applicants per vacancy are lower, so you have higher chances.

For example for "project coordinator" the number of applicants may be high, but for "buyer assistant" it can be lower. So competition is less while jobs are similar.

2. Make 3-4 applications per day, while slightly modifying your resume to have the same keywords as the job description

Simply select the 3-4 best options from today's set of vacancies. Do not overthink it: just make 3-4 applications. It is better to be one of the first applicants, so just apply for fresh vacancies. There is no need to catch up with the whole history of LinkedIn.

3. Try to spend 1.5 hours max, and when you are done just forget about it till tomorrow and enjoy your day. Adjust the top 30% of your resume and add the keywords which are relevant to the job description, so when somebody reads it, it feels like you are the right candidate.

Do not put a lot of hope on one single application. Maybe out of 50 applications you will get 1 or 2 interviews, and that's ok.

4. Employers always select from the available sample. Your job is to get to the sample where you are the best option:

- a) of the resumes/profiles submitted
- b) of the interviewees.

5. Do not get emotionally involved. Just do the numbers.

If you have persistence and determination you will make it.

The next chapter is focused on resumes, so I will only mention a couple of things here. During the application process, the role of a resume is to get you an interview. Normally people do not spend a lot of time reading a resume; they scan the top 30% of it, and if they find relevant keywords, names, or numbers there then they continue. You need to make sure that what you have in the top 30% of the first page of your resume has matching keywords vs job description, as well as big numbers and recognizable brands, so the recruiter will read further. Keep this in mind.

6. Make sure that the company you are applying to is on the list of companies who can apply for your work permit via a simplified procedure (sponsorship). Normally this list is published on the website of the Immigration and Naturalization office.

- At the end of the year (November, December), the demand is low
- At the beginning of the year (February, March), companies have new budgets and demand is higher.
- Check if somebody you know is already working in the company and can send a reference letter to HR. If you completed an MBA,

check where alumni got their jobs. Find people with a similar background (country of origin, current location, job function) and see where they are working now. It will give you an idea of which companies can hire people like you.

7. If you do not speak the local language, look for international companies which are not focused on the local market, but rather supply globally. Then it is more likely that they have expats like you.

WHERE TO LOOK FOR A JOB

1. LinkedIn

LinkedIn is a great channel to look for a job. Check new positions daily. Also, update your profile to make sure recruiters can find you.

Key criteria to be searchable on LinkedIn are:

Current & Previous Position Title

Weighted very high. This is your most important field and I would strongly recommend that you use the 100 characters to their full potential. Don't just say "project manager"; you should include as many keywords as possible to describe your position

Location

Make sure that your location is set to where you want to find a job

Company Name

When you add a company where you worked previously, select it from LinkedIn's auto-fill options; otherwise, when a recruiter is using advanced search and filters down to see who has worked at a certain company, you will not be shown in the results.

Connections count

Make sure that you have as many connections as you can. In Linkedin's search algorithm, a moderate weight seems to be placed on the people who are closest to you. Proactively reach out to recruiters and connect with them.

Profile completion percentage, Professional picture, etc.

Regarding the language, if you are applying to an international company and your position is not focused on the local market then fluent English is enough. It is also a good sign if the vacancy is written in English.

In the long term, it is good to master the language, but in the short term, you will not be able to speak fluently to get a "local market-focused" position.

Examples (NL – global focus): Philips, AkzoNobel, ASML, Shell

Examples (NL – local focus): KPN, Albert Heijn, Rabobank

2. Recruiting agencies

Normally there are 2-3 really big agencies (like Michael Page or Hays), and many smaller agencies.

Do not be shy: contact many recruiters and share your profile. If you make a good first impression, they might invite you to an interview, even if there is no position, or there are temporary roles that you can fill while looking for a permanent job.

3. Regional or country-specific resources

Normally it is more than enough to use LinkedIn, but you can also Google if there are strong regional websites.

To summarize:

1. A job is not an ideal way to make money, but it is good to have a job at the beginning, to pay your bills and have a legal reason to stay in the country
2. You need to have a strong motivation to stay and should not have any plan B
3. Getting a job is about luck, and to deal with luck you need to make many attempts until you get lucky.
4. Establish a regular process by submitting 3-4 resumes every day, slightly adjusting the top 30% to match the keywords with the job description.
5. Do some research and understand where people with similar profiles and background (expats) got their jobs
6. Use a mix of LinkedIn, recruiting agencies, and country-specific sites.
7. Do not get involved emotionally: do not forget to eat well, sleep long enough, and exercise.
8. There is a 100% chance that you will make it if you really want it.

CV

The primary function of a resume is to get you an interview.

Nobody is going to read your resume. They going to scan it for 10 seconds, so make sure that all the important stuff is in the top 30% of the first page.

There are 3 things employers are looking for in the resume:

Keywords that are similar to what is in the job description

- Customize your resume and add the keywords from the vacancy
- Focus on the top 30% of the first page
- Recruiters/HR scan your resume, and if they do not see the keywords, they will simply read another resume

Sexy big brands or impressive numbers

- If you were not working at Fortune-500 companies, maybe you were doing some projects for these companies. Words like "Coca-Cola", "HSBC" or "Samsung" are very helpful.
- If you were working with big budgets or projects it is good to mention these. Recruiters are going to read plenty of resumes, so yours needs to stand out

Function and industry-related experience

- Function first, industry second. If they are looking for a procurement manager, they won't be interested in your experience in Marketing Communications
- Do not change both at the same time: function and industry
- Employers want to minimize their risk, not to maximize it

Also, it is important to have a good template and structure, so they can easily read it.

Some recommendations:

Remove everything that doesn't add value and put everything that adds value to the top of the first page

Do not make a regionally focused resume (Vietnam, India, Philippines, etc.)

- Do not mention your full name if it is too long and difficult to pronounce
- Do not overemphasize experience in one country if it is not your target country or the EU
- Do not mention languages that are not relevant for the job (Hindi, Arabic, etc.), and do not put your home country next to each position, as it can put your ability to work in an international company into question

Do not be shy

- Change "English advanced" to "Fluent"
- Remember to mention all the awards you had in the past
- Make things slightly bigger than they actually are (without lying)

Mention your achievements, not only responsibilities. Be specific, where it adds value.

INTERVIEW

The interview is an opportunity to get a job. There are many interviews and many opportunities. Do not put all your stakes on one interview – consider it a regular activity, like when you go to the gym. You can practice, do your best, and maybe you will win the medal, or maybe not. Both are ok.

Depending on the company you will have 2 or 3 interviews. The corporate world is about reducing risks, so people want to share the risk of making a decision.

Your first interview will most likely be with HR or directly with the hiring manager. They can bring one more colleague to the table. And your second interview could be with the boss of the hiring manager.

The standard process is:

- HR (they first call you to check the red flags and plan a face-to-face interview)
- Hiring manager + HR
- Senior manager or future team
- HR – contract details

During the interview, they will focus on your experience and your personality.

Basically, they want to get answers to four main questions:

Can you do the job?

Are you a good fit for this job, do you have knowledge and skills, and have you done something similar before?

Do they like you as a person?

It is about fitting in with the team and your future boss. They will only hire you if they like you. The best way to make them like you is to listen more and to show that you like them as people. People normally like those who like them, who laugh at their jokes, who say "it is a very good question", "you are absolutely right, it is a very good observation" and so on.

Can you fit into the existing team and influence internal stakeholders to get things done?

Are you persistent and motivated? Do you have positive energy? Can you convince stakeholders and push things forward? To have topic-related knowledge is not enough; you should be able to get things done and manage your stakeholders.

Red flags

Is anything wrong with you that means they should not hire you?

INTERVIEW STRATEGY

There are some simple strategies that will help you during the interview

1.

Do not make any interview important. Assume you won't get the job. Just go and talk to them, practice, as if preparing for your next interview. People like candidates who want a job but do not need it. You should be interested but not needy.

2.

To calm down your nerves, do 3 things:
- Exercise before the interview, so your body is not tense
- Eat something to make yourself heavier
- If you are still nervous - you can consider taking a daily recommended dose of magnesium (not medical advice, check with doctor if necessary).

And remember, you are only nervous for the first 5 minutes of the interview, and it is actually not fear, but rather excitement. To get through the first five minutes just ask a question and let them talk while you are adjusting to the situation.

3.

At the beginning of the interview let them introduce the job, for example by asking them to say a bit more about the job profile so you can better understand what is important. Then start answering their questions based on what they said earlier.

It is much better if they talk first, so you can get an idea of who they are, what are they looking for, and what is important for this role. Then your answers will be in line with what they just said.

4.

All your answers should focus on two things:

- Why you are a good fit for this job
- How much you like them

Why you are a good fit for this job

For example, when they ask you about your weaknesses, you can say something like: "I am a very detail-oriented person, sometimes to extremes. For example, once I checked the file 3 times before sending it to the client and I only noticed a mistake when I checked it a second time. But I think for somebody working in the reporting team it is a rather good quality, because the information we are sharing will be audited later, and any mistake can be misinterpreted."

Or if they ask you about your experience, do not talk about stuff not related to the job description; only focus on experiences that make you a good candidate for this job.

How much you like them

It's very simple: People like those who like them (at least in work-related situations).. Therefore at least for the length of the interview, you need to find something you really like in people who interview you. And then you should speak to this part as much as you can. Start your answers with:

- This is a very good question
- I fully agree with what you just said
- You just put it so nicely
- I cannot agree more
- I was thinking exactly the same thing
- As you rightly said earlier
- I also like it
- It is also my favorite

Make them feel liked; people hire people they want to work with. And normally people want to work with somebody who likes them a lot.

To summarize:

- Do not make any of the interviews very important, as it will only make you stressed. Consider it a training session and assume that you won't get the job. It will make you relaxed
- Exercise, eat, consider taking daily recommended dose of magnesium
- Focus on the 4 key questions
- Figure out how to fall in love with people who interview you, at least for the time of the interview
- Interview is about making them interested, more than about expressing a lot of interest yourself

SALARY AND CONTRACT CONDITIONS

Normally in European companies, each position has a certain grade and each grade has a range of salaries, from 60% to 110%.

For example, if your grade is A, your salary range is between € 75 and 100K. Of course, the range and grades differ per company, but it is important to understand how salaries are structured.

There are also additional payments, but we will talk about them later.

Let's start from concept #1:

The job you are applying for can belong to one or two grades (for example Grade 4 and Grade 5). And within these grades, there is a range of possible salaries. When negotiating a salary your job is to figure out this range and get the highest possible %. There is no fixed salary for a position. There is a range, and you need to be as close to the upper limit of the range as possible.

Do not give a simple answer: "I want X". If you want € 50K but the actual range is € 70-90K, you will be perceived as underqualified. Ask what grade this position belongs to and what the salary range is within this grade.

Also remember, the more they pay you, the more they appreciate and respect you because then you are a more expensive resource. If they really like you, it is ok to express your concerns about their initial proposal and ask what the possibilities are.

Just to give you some reference, in our group the lowest salary was around € **40-45K gross**, and the highest around € **95K gross**.

Another important point is to understand the structure of the package. Sometimes additional items can be very substantial and can easily compensate for a lower salary.

The package can include bonus, vacation allowance (almost a month's salary), vacation days + leave days (and sometimes there is an opportunity to sell some of your leave days and get money).

Example of a pay package

- **Salary:** 12 months + 8% holiday allowance (can be paid monthly or once a year)
  For net check net salary calculator
- **EBITDA bonus** (0-8%) 45-50% tax – the amount depends on the company performance
- **Performance bonus** (0-5%) 50% tax
- **XX vacation days**

Sometimes bonuses can be combined and be up to 12-15% of the yearly salary.

You can also get a company car or extra payment per month if your grade is high enough.

Some examples of salary negotiation:

Ask them: what is the salary range for this grade? This way you refer to their policies and avoid random discussions about what the right salary is. They can only give you a salary within their range; everything else doesn't matter.

Or you can say that you would like to get a proposal based on the salary range and their evaluation of your profile.

If you need to give a number, give something 15%-20% above your expectations and say that first of all you are interested in this role and the salary is negotiable.

In most situations, whoever discloses information first is at a disadvantage

Ask in detail about all conditions. Sometimes you can compensate for a lower salary with extra paid vacation days, or a travel allowance, company car, bonus, etc.

It is very important to negotiate a good grade and a good salary at the beginning. Because normally an annual salary increase is low, and promotion to the next grade takes a few years. So if your starting point is low, it will take a while to get to a better situation.

Remember, you are talking about 2-10 years of your life when you are negotiating your salary and grade, so do not take it easy, get as much as you can, and do not be shy. Ask questions. Let them make the first offer. Do not accept the first offer unless you really like it. Ask for a better offer. They already invested time in you, and in the end, they are not spending their own money, so plus or minus € 10K is not a big deal for them.

Moving to Europe as an Expat

FIRST YEAR IN THE COMPANY

When you start a new job you need to:
- Make a good first impression
- Build your network & identify key stakeholders
- Understand the business
- Identify a few important topics you need to focus on to make an impact

Always remember that perception and visibility are as important in the corporate world as the job itself. It is never only about the task at hand and achieving results.

Equation of successful corporate career is:
- People & communication skills – 40%
- Perception and storytelling – 40%
- Understanding of politics – 10%
- Luck – 10%

Use extended teams or agencies / consultants as leverage to achieve the results. Of course, it depends on your position. If you are an engineer or somebody in IT you probably need to do hands-on tasks as well.

In any case, learn how to present, how to convince people, how to build alliances, and how to manage individual contributors and teams who will help to achieve the results.

A good start is:

1. **Focus on key issues and key people.** Understand big issues your team or company is focused on and figure out how you can contribute. First of all, understand the top-3 priorities of your boss and figure out how you can contribute.

2. **Spend time with people and be visible.** Meet a lot of people, send a lot of emails. Talk about important topics. Make your team, your boss, and your business visible.

3. **Get leverage** in terms of people or budget.

4. **Have the right attitude.** When you work, enjoy what you do, be enthusiastic, give compliments to people, and create excitement.

5. **Learn how to present, how to communicate, how to connect to people, and how to tell the story.** The higher you climb, the less content you need to produce – it will be produced by people working for you, or agencies. What you need is to point them in the right direction and tell the story – the story that will contribute to the story of people above you.

HOW TO SUCCEED IN
THE CORPORATE WORLD

1. Make sure you know the top-3 priorities of your boss and their boss, and then figure out how you can contribute. Always link what you do to the strategy and objectives of your boss. If it is not aligned with the strategy or objectives of your boss, simply stop doing it.

2. Spend an equal amount of time on the job itself and communication / visibility / building your network and relations with people.

3. Your energy level and your attitude define your performance. Exercise, eat, sleep, and always find a positive angle on any situation.

4. Get leverage in terms of people or budget, to run bigger projects and create impact.

5. Create enough empty space in your schedule to think and reflect, start keeping a journal, or go for a half-day walk – whatever works best for you. Empty your head and then think about one or two important questions. For example: what works best and gets appreciated? Or what takes most of your time and produces negligible results? Do more of what works and eliminate activities that are not important. Ideally, your schedule should consist of one or two tasks every day. Deep work produces better results, comparing to jumping from one meeting to another, unless these are meetings to brief your resources (agencies,

direct reports) or present to senior management.

6. Take long vacations, recharge, and create empty space, hunger and curiosity.

Performance = energy * leverage * where you apply it. If any of these are close to zero, it won't work. If you do not have energy, there is nothing you can do. If you have a lot of energy but no leverage, you will create a negligible impact. If you have a lot of energy and a lot of leverage but apply it in the wrong direction – you will get a negative result. Think about it.

PART VI:
BUYING A HOUSE

HOW TO CHOOSE A HOUSE

First of all, let me tell you why you should buy a house instead of renting one.

I will give you an example.

For a few years, I was renting a 20 sq. m. studio in Utrecht, Netherlands for around € 1.2K per month. It was a small, one-room place with shared stairs/entrance.

My monthly rent simply disappeared from my account without creating any long-term value.

Then I applied for a mortgage and bought a house. It was 10-year-old 3-floor 90 sq. m. brick house with a separate entrance and roof terrace. The price of the house was € 315K.

I took 30-year mortgage with a 20-year fixed interest rate of 2.68% ,which is quite high nowadays.

It means that every month I have to pay € 1.2K to the bank.

- Part of this amount goes to a down payment, building assets for me
- Interest payment is tax-deductible, and you can apply for advanced re-payments, so I receive about 200 euros per month from the tax administration

- In 2 years the price of my house has increased by more than €100K, so if I sold it and started renting again, I would make around €120K profit (including price increase and down payment).

As a result:

- I have a house 4 times the size of the place I rented
- I pay 200 euros less per month
- I own the place and build my assets
- I feel more settled because I have my own place

Of course, it can be a bit scary to take out a €300K+ debt. But think about it this way: you can always sell it, pay back, and start renting again. Also in some countries (like in NL), there is a program where you can insure the price of your house. You pay something like 1% of the price (one-off payment) and then in case the price of your house goes down when you want to sell it, the insurance will pay the bank the difference between the selling price and the mortgage. Basically, it eliminates all risks and makes the idea of buying a house very attractive.

Now about choosing a house.

There are different strategies, depending on the market situation and your personality type. Some people are willing to buy something half-cooked and renovate it, some are willing to wait for a new project to be completed, and some simply want to move in and start living somewhere with what is already available.

Irrespective of your preferences, you should consider the following:

Future value of the house

A house is an investment. See it this way. You need to evaluate how likely it that its future price will outperform the market, no matter in which direction the market moves.

Of course, the most important factor is location. Just think: when somebody says they bought a house, your first question is always: "where?". Location really is the key. A house in the city center or in a popular area will always outperform the market.

- How close is it to the station and to the city center?
- How well connected by public transportation is it?
- What kind of neighborhood is it? Is it one of the best neighborhoods in the city?
- Does it have shops, a sports center, GP, and a park nearby?

It is also important if you want to rent it out in the future. People prefer to rent nice places in nice neighborhoods. No surprise.

Condition of the house

- How old is it?
- How much do you need to invest to make it livable?
- Does all the basic infrastructure function properly (pipes, gas, electricity)?
- What is the energy level?

Red flags

For example, a school close to a playground for kids that create a lot of noise during the day, or steep stairs (not suitable for people with kids or older people), or a highway, railway or cemetery nearby: all these factors will influence the likelihood of selling the house for a good price. Do not only think about yourself when you buy a house (maybe you can easily cope with noise), but think about the people who will view it later, when you want to sell it.

Another thing you want to check is whether the land is fully owned or rented from the municipality.

Your emotions

Another really important question is, how do you feel about buying this house? Do you feel excited, unsure, or even doubtful?

There is a simple rule – only buy a house if you really, really like it and can't wait to move in.

Remember, you will need to take out a huge debt and pay it for a long time, plus invest in renovation and furniture. Only excitement will give you enough energy to get it done and live a happy life there. Your emotions are reflections of small observations, sometimes not detected by your brain, but they are equally important.

Calibrate

View at least 10 houses to get a better idea of what you like, what you don't like, and how houses compare with each other. It really helps to calibrate your eye so you can make a good judgment after viewing the house.

In terms of the search process, the steps are usually as follows:

Mortgage advisor

Normally, even before making appointments and looking for a house, you should meet with a mortgage advisor, bring a couple of documents (mainly your salary slip) so they can calculate your maximum mortgage, and confirm that there will be no issues to get it.

You should explain your situation in detail, to make sure the process will go smoothly. A mortgage advisor normally takes a fixed fee of about € 2,5K. You can also apply for a mortgage yourself, but the bank will charge around € 1K in this case anyway. So it is probably better if somebody does the work for you, for the extra fee. However, it is not a must. It all depends on your level of comfort.

House search: you can search for the house yourself or hire a makelaar (realtor)

Makelaar

Normally you only need a makelaar (realtor) if the market in a certain city is very hot. They charge around € 1.5-3K. Some of them will select houses and invite you to the viewing, some will ask you to select houses online yourself and then they will join you to give their feedback and help estimate the price and negotiate.

Their selling points are:

- They know the market and can suggest an optimal bidding price
- They know each other and put their reputation on the line during the sale process (in front of other makelaars), hence a selling makelaar will always choose a buyer with a makelaar (not true), to make sure that the deal goes through
- They have the information about new houses before they are published on the market

I am not a big believer in makelaars when you buy a house. I think every seller wants to maximize the number of offers and get the highest price and therefore will make the house publicly available anyway. And in order to evaluate the optimal bidding price, you can use online resources. It is ok to use a makelaar if you have extra money, but it should be possible to do it yourself as well.

Where to search for a house

Normally there is one big platform in the country where most of the houses are published. Just figure out what it is in your country and use it. You should be able to search by city and postcode, with various filters like price, square meters, etc.

It is important to contact sellers as soon as possible, especially if the market is hot. Figure out when they publish new listings and call to make appointments right away.

Appointment

Normally there are two types of appointments:

- Open house: everyone can visit on a certain date within a given timeframe
- Individual appointment

Make a lot of appointments, go and view the house, list your criteria in advance, and check if the house matches these criteria.

Offer

Ask when the deadline is to submit an offer. Normally you need to send it via email, stating your offered price and conditions. See the example of the proposal below.

Dear XXX,

I viewed the house (address) last Saturday and I would like to make an offer.

*I can offer **315,000** euros for this house.*

I need 2.5 weeks to arrange the mortgage (I already had a discussion with my mortgage advisor and provided all the necessary documents). Regarding the date to receive the keys, I am flexible: any time between May and September is ok.

About me: I am an expat, living in the Netherlands for 5 years (permanent residence). For the last 4 years I have been working as a Digital Marketing Manager at XXX (Dutch multinational company) on a permanent contract. Currently, I rent a place in Utrecht city center, and I would like to buy a house so I have my own place.

If you have any questions or need any further information, please feel free to contact me.

When considering your proposal, they only care about two things:

- Maximum bid
- Degree of certainty that you will finalize the deal (get the mortgage, complete the purchase)

Additionally, check the rules in your country. In NL, offers are not binding.

Signing preliminary agreement

If your offer is accepted, you will soon sign a preliminary agreement. It also depends on the country. In NL, even after signing the agreement you have a 3-day cooling-off period when you can cancel without any explanation, but after 3 days it is legally binding and you must proceed with the purchase or pay a fine if you decide to cancel.

Finalizing the mortgage

After signing the preliminary agreement you need to arrange a mortgage. Normally it takes 2-3 weeks. There is already a date planned to sign a transfer deed, so make sure you organize your mortgage on time.

Transfer agreement

Together with the seller you visit the notary and sign two papers.

- Mortgage documents (notary signs it on behalf of the bank)
- Transfer deed

Then your name is added to the register, you receive the keys and the house is yours.

There is a bill for this process.

The new law says that if you are below 35 years old and buying your first house, you do not have to pay 2% tax.

Do not be too worried about the whole thing: millions of people bought their houses by getting a mortgage, it is a very standard process, and if you use common sense nothing can go wrong. Only do what you understand, what you like and feel happy about. There might be slight discomfort when borrowing a large amount of money, but please rationalize it. The house is the guarantee of your loan, so in the worst case scenario you will sell your house and start renting again. It is not a big risk.

HOW TO APPLY FOR A MORTGAGE

Normally in Europe, you only need a few documents:

1. Passport
2. Your three most recent salary slips
3. Employer statement (that you are working and are a permanent employee).

If you are an entrepreneur, you need to show consistent income over a certain period of time

4. Highly skilled migrant residence card, or permanent residence card and passport

The classical route is to meet with the bank or with a mortgage advisor, share your situation and your documents and ask them to check: a) if you are eligible for a mortgage, and b) what is the maximum mortgage you can get.

In the Netherlands, banks will charge you around € 1K extra for all services, and mortgage advisors will charge around € 2.5K. In my view it is better to have a mortgage advisor, as he or she will be fully dedicated to your case, while the bank basically will charge you € 1K for nothing, won't look for a better offer somewhere else, and won't add any additional value to what you could have done yourself.

After you get a confirmation from the mortgage advisor that you can get a mortgage, and also when you know your maximum, you can start looking for a house and start bidding.

If you have extra money, of course you can pay on top of your mortgage or take less money from the bank.

When your bid is accepted, you need to arrange a mortgage within 2-3 weeks.

Your advisor offers you 2-3 options, which depend on:

- How long you want to fix the interest rate. The longer it is fixed, the higher your rate is, but then you also have more certainty about what you are going to pay. Normally 10 or 20 years fixed interest is ok.
- What type of mortgage you want (annuity etc.)

They will submit your documents to the bank and let you know when the mortgage has been approved. Normally it is all via the internet, and you do not need to see anybody in person.

You will sign mortgage documents at the notary right before signing the transfer deed for the house.

Then two things happen:

- You start paying monthly to the bank
- The bank forgets about you while you continue paying the mortgage

For example, they don't care if you change your job or quit or do something else, as long as they receive the money.

A mortgage is a good thing. It is better to own a house than to rent one. But this is the only debt you should have as a physical person. You can borrow money for your business as a legal entity, but do not borrow money for anything else personally. Spend less than you earn.

BIDDING

Probably there is no simple rule in bidding, as it really depends on the market and specific situation. However, let me share some thoughts.

Seller's or buyer's market

First of all, you need to know that in most cases in Europe it is either a seller's market or a buyer's market. If it is a seller's market then you need to bid above the asking price to get a house; if it is a buyer's market you can bid below the asking price.

In the Netherlands, it is a seller's market.

For example, for a house with an asking price of € 300K, you can easily bid anything between € 305K and € 350K to get the house, and it still won't guarantee anything.

From the seller's perspective, they care about two things:

- Getting the highest possible price
- Having the highest confidence that the deal will go through (that you will get the mortgage, etc.)

When bidding, keep in mind that the bank will only give you money for the market value of the house (i.e., an expert's calculation about the actual market value of the house). So you need to figure out what the market value of your house is. If you bid above the market value, you need to cover the difference from your own pocket.

Confidence in your offer

Regarding the second point, the seller has the highest possible confidence if you pay the full amount in cash (no loan). But it is unlikely.

So it is important to tell them that you had a mortgage screening and got confirmation that you can get a loan.

If you are buying your first house and do not need to sell another house first it is also an advantage, as you are not in a chain, and so there are fewer pitfalls.

Mentioning that you have been working for a well-known company for several years and have a steady income also helps.

Normally you need to submit your bid by a certain date and time via email. Make sure you know the conditions in your country, e.g. if the bid is legally binding or not.

In the Netherlands, your offer is only legally binding when you sign a preliminary agreement, and you still have a 3-day cooling-off period when you can cancel it without any explanations. After that, you will have to pay a cancellation fee, which can be anything between 5-10% of the price of the house.

Regarding the bid itself, how much should you bid?

There are nice online platforms where you can check the selling prices of the houses in that area for a reasonable fee, as well as get an estimated bidding range. For example https://www.calcasa.nl/

See their report in appendix

The price for the report at the time of writing this book was around 30 euros. So if you bid for 3-5 houses, you might spend 30-150 euros.

In my case, I bid 5% above the asking price and had a check with my mortgage advisor upfront to get a rough estimate of the market value of the house, to make sure I could get a 100% mortgage.

No matter how hot the market is, I would never overbid too much, because then you will get what is called "buyer's punishment" – paying an unreasonable price.

If houses in your target area are too expensive, try to add more areas where demand is less, but that are still well connected to the city center and have good infrastructure. If you focus on one area, you can get too anxious. If you consider 4-5 areas, you will have more options, it will cool you down a bit and make you more pragmatic. When I was house hunting, I heard many comments that there was no chance of buying a house unless you overbid a lot. But anyway I always placed reasonable bids, had around 10 rejections, but then ended up with two accepted offers and had to choose the one I liked the most.

Stay mentally tough, rational, and prepare to play the long game. It is better to buy a good house in 1 year than get anxious and get stuck with a house you bought too quickly.

Bidding letter

Here's an example of the bidding letter:

Dear XXX,

I viewed the house (address) last Saturday and I would like to make an offer.

*I can offer **315,000** euros for this house. [Comment: of course the key in your offer is the bidding price].*

I need 2.5 weeks to arrange the mortgage (I already had a discussion with my mortgage advisor and provided all necessary documents). [Here you signal that you are fully confident in your ability to get the mortgage and already had a check with the advisor].

Regarding the date to receive the keys, I am flexible: any time between May and September is ok.

About me: I am an expat, living in the Netherlands for 5 years (permanent residence). For the last 4 years I have been working as a Digital Marketing Manager in XXX (Dutch multinational company) on a permanent contract. Currently, I rent a place in Utrecht city center, and I would like to buy a house so I have my own place. [Here you signal that you do not need to sell another house before buying this one, so you are not in a chain].

If you have any questions or need any further information – please feel free to contact me.

You can also mention conditions – subject to mortgage approval, house inspection, etc. Of course, each condition will reduce the attractiveness of your offer. But still, do not remove what you do not feel comfortable removing. For example, I removed "subject to mortgage approval" because my advisor said that there was a 99.99% chance that I would get the mortgage, so I felt comfortable risking 0.01%.

And again, when buying a house in a seller's market, luck plays a big role, so maximize the number of options, and do not bet everything on one house.

Your objective is to get a good house for a good price, not a specific house for an unreasonable price.

HOUSE INSPECTION

I do not have a lot of experience with the house inspection, since my house was relatively new, approximately 10 years old. But if it is an old house, you should hire somebody to do a house inspection and give you a report with their findings. If there are some material issues, you might want to reduce the bidding price.

This technical inspection provides you with information regarding the technical condition of the house and its structures. This assessment will also alert you to shortcomings and defects.

Check if the company can provide the report in English so you can understand the details and use them in your negotiation.

SIGNING A CONTRACT

You got the mortgage confirmation and now is the date when you will sign the contract and get a house.

Normally, the seller selects the notary.

You need to transfer all the fees to complete the deed at the notary in advance.

After that, all you need to do is to go there on a certain date and time with your passport and probably with your residence card.

The process takes around 30 minutes.

If you do not speak the local language, there will be an interpreter and of course, it will be added to your bill.

Normally you have to pay for:

- Interpreter
- Notary
- Transfer tax (depends on the country but let's say 2% of the value of the house)
- Cost of the mortgage advisor

So if you bought a house for € 300K you will pay something like € 10K.

If you qualify you can also take National guarantee insurance (1% of the house value) which will cover the difference between the buying price and the market price of the house, in case you need to sell it (because you cannot pay the mortgage). So basically it will ensure that you won't have to pay anything extra if you are forced to sell the house and its market value has gone down.

Normally if your house qualifies for a National mortgage guarantee you will get a lower interest rate, because the bank has lower risk and therefore can offer a better interest rate.

Check if there is something similar in your country.

All in all, in NL the total fees will be somewhere between € 10K and € 20K, depending on the value of your house. There are some exceptions, for example, people below 35 years old who are buying their first house do not have to pay 2% transfer tax.

When you are at the notary, you sign the mortgage deed first. From this moment you owe something like € 300K to the bank. Congrats!

Then you sign a transfer deed and now you own a house. Then the seller gives you the key and that's it. It's really nothing special; just signing a couple of papers.

The notary will take care of:

- Paying the transfer tax
- Paying the mortgage advisor
- Receiving the money from the bank and transferring it to the seller
- Making a change in the registry and transferring house ownership to you

Then you shake hands and leave the notary with the keys in your pocket and with a debt of at least €300K+.

But do not worry.

Buying a house is really nothing more than renting it from the bank.

With some important benefits:

1. Now it is your house and the landlord cannot kick you out, because there is no landlord.

2. Part of what you pay to the bank is a down payment, which means you start building assets, and when you sell the house this part belongs to you. Remember, when you rent, you do not build any assets, but just throw the money away.

3. A house can go up in price, and when you sell it you can make a profit (unless you buy a bigger house which will also go up in price).

4. Normally the amount of your monthly payment to the bank allows you to buy a better and bigger house than what you could have rented with the same amount. For example, you can pay € 1.2K rent for a 40 sq. m. studio or a 1-bedroom apartment or the same € 1.2K as a mortgage payment for an 80-90 sq. m. apartment/house. So with the same monthly cost, you can get a much better place, and part of this monthly payment will be your asset, which you can recover if you sell the house later.

5. Additionally, at least at the moment, the interest you pay to the bank is tax-deductible, so you can get something like 200 euros monthly back, which brings your total monthly payment down to € 1K.

6. Some of the transaction costs are also tax-deductible, hence after paying € 10-15K you can recover something like € 2-4K after submitting your annual tax return.

7. You feel more settled when you have your own house. It is a small, but important addition.

All in all, a house is the only item worth taking a loan for, and it is a financially sound decision to buy a house instead of renting one.

No matter how big it sounds, it is a really normal and standard process, and almost nothing can go wrong. Do not be afraid, banks know what they are doing and won't give you a loan unless they have sufficient confidence that you can pay it.

I never imagined myself buying something so expensive, but it is really not such a big deal: just make a poker face and take it easy.

Many people have been there, done it, and are totally ok now.

The concept of Europe is to make sure that basic things are easy to get for everyone. And then they use huge tax scissors to make sure you won't get more than average and use this extra they chop from you to distribute among those who cannot earn it themselves.

After buying a house get a glass of wine to celebrate your small victory and move to the next goal, as a house is just a place where you live, where you store your books and shoes, and where you put together your ambitious plans. One day those plans will come true, if you work hard, if you do not complain and if you do not allow yourself to have any excuses.

MOVING IN, RENOVATION, SETTLING DOWN

Of course, it all depends on the house you bought.

But here are some thoughts on moving in & settling down.

If you bought a relatively new house with an ok kitchen and bathroom, and you do not have to change the floor and stuff, then putting in some basic furniture, light and equipment will cost anything between € 10K and € 15K.

You can choose to buy items from Ikea or combine items from different stores. Just one suggestion: do not strive for completion. If you cannot afford to buy the stuff you really like in one go, do not buy mediocre items, take more time and only buy things you really like and would want to move with you to your next house.

I made this mistake and bought some ok sofa, rugs, bookshelves or lamps that I later had to replace with items I liked more.

Your house is your place of power. It should make you feel happy, successful, and inspired. Surround yourself with items that you really love and that make you feel good. It is important.

Some simple rules for arranging your house:

Rule 1: Use odd numbers and shapes

Space is more visually appealing when there are an odd number of objects in it. Odd numbers create light asymmetry, making the area more interesting for the eye. It is also good to group items of different heights, shapes, and textures. At the same time, there should be something similar about them, for example, theme or color.

Rule 2: Keep the 60-30-10 ratio when choosing colors

You should choose a dominant color, a secondary color, and an accent color. The dominant color should cover 60% of the room and be rather neutral (white, light blue, light green). Normally this is the color of the walls and ceiling or the color of the floor. The secondary color can be brighter and bolder; most often it is the color of the furniture. This should cover around 30% of the room. The last one, accent color, is used for accessories such as rugs and cushions and makes up the remaining 10%.

Rule 3: Create a negative space

A negative space is an area free of any objects. You need to deliberately create empty space so the items in the room can breathe and present themselves with confidence. A single red rose looks best on a white background, not with a bunch of flowers of all different kinds.

Rule 4: Define a focal point

In the room, there should be a focal point that immediately draws attention. It could be a big painting, a fireplace or a beautiful antique chair. The rest of the space should be arranged around the focal point, elegantly complementing it.

If your space is rather tight, use mirrors to make it look bigger.

Dare to use big mirrors

Large mirrors work especially well in a small space because they create the illusion of depth and make a small room feel bigger. Mirrors are also great for narrow spots such as hallways.

Think about the reflection

When hanging a mirror think about what it will reflect. When placed correctly, mirrors can highlight a focal point of the room or an important architectural detail. It is also a good idea to hang a mirror across from a window. It will make a room brighter and livelier.

Choose the right style

Depending on the frame, mirrors can be classic, modern, vintage, and so on. Consider the style of the room when choosing a mirror in a frame to create a match – or maybe a contradiction!

To make your house livelier you can also add some plants or plant-inspired motifs.

Floor plants for large rooms with empty space

If your room has an abundance of empty space, a floor plant can be the ideal solution. If you noticed that some spots in your house do not feel complete, a couple of floor plants could be the missing ingredient to make them look fresh.

Cut blooms to add different colors every week

Replacing cut flowers can be a great way to change the look of your room without too much expense or effort. It is an easy option to add some new colors to your home.

Hanging plants for wall decoration

With small planters, you can keep a variety of herbs in your kitchen that will beautify the space and add freshness to your cooking.

Decorative items with floral motifs

If taking care of plants is too complicated, but you still want to add some green motifs to your home, a large-scale mural with a plant motif or cushions that include a floral ornament will give you a sense of having plants around.

Make sure you have a couple of statement pieces in your living room and your master bedroom.

When you decorate your house, you attempt to organize an orchestra from various items, so they play a nice and sophisticated melody together. However, sometimes they need to be quiet and let one of them play solo.

Think carefully: which of the items in the room will be your statement piece? It can be an antique dining table, a colorful rug, or a sparkling chandelier. No matter what it is, for the statement piece size matters – to capture the attention it needs to be bigger than other items in the room.

Another important topic is lighting. Ideally, the room should have layered lighting to create a nice vibe. Therefore, you can consider mixing different types of lights – table lamps, chandeliers, wall sconces, and so on.

One of the options is to use light as an art object and acquire a beautiful wall light that will replace a painting and serve as a conversation starter when you invite your guests over.

Another idea would be to buy an oversized arched floor lamp with a sharp silhouette, which will become a statement item in your living room. This lamp can be considered as a beautiful piece of furniture during the day and as a chic source of illumination in the evening.

Don't be afraid to mix different styles to spice things up, for example, by introducing vintage sconces to a contemporary living room or adding contemporary lighting to a classic design. Or you can create an intentional mismatch instead of pairing light items. It is more pleasing on the eye to see the dynamic environment with elements that create a movement, instead of perfectly balanced and sterilized symmetries.

Also do not forget that windows are important sources of light during the day, and by placing a mirror opposite a window you can make the room brighter.

Finally, nothing compares with fire and cracks of wood. If space allows, a fireplace would be a perfect source of light in the living room, especially during the winter. If you are not lucky enough to have this, you can replace it with candlesticks of different styles and materials to brighten the atmosphere in the evening.

TAX RETURN

Currently, in the Netherlands (please check regulations of your country) there are two types of mortgage-related costs which are tax-deductible:

1. Transfer tax (approx. 2% of the price of your house)
2. The interest you pay to the bank

Transfer tax

After you pay the bill to transfer the house, part of this bill is tax-deductible, which can be reflected in your annual tax statement. As a result, you will get some money back from the tax office (around € 2-4K, depending on the price of your house).

For example, if you bought a house in August, next year around March you can submit your annual statement, and then around May-June you can get the money from the tax office.

Interest

Interest can be deducted in two ways:

- You can reflect it in the annual statement, hence it is deducted from your income, your income becomes lower and the tax office has to pay back some of the tax they collected from you with the assumption that your income was higher. In this case, you will receive money back on an annual basis, sometime around May or June. For example, for a house of € 300K it can be something like € 2.5K annually.

- You can apply for a preliminary tax return on a monthly basis. In this case, the tax office will return this tax in advance on a monthly basis, and then you need to do a final calculation in your annual statement. For example, for a house of around € 300K it can be something like € 200 per month. This is just an indication to give you some idea; it can be different in your country.

The point here is that you need to check what can be deducted from your income and what are tax benefits of buying a house in your country. Maybe they are similar, or maybe there are none. But if they do exist, you should apply for them to minimize your costs and return some of your investments in the house.

Normally you can apply yourself online, or hire a tax advisor (which I did). In my case, he charged about 120 euros for the first statement (where I deducted the transfer tax) and then about 60 euros for annual statements.

PART VII:
PERMANENT RESIDENCE OR PASSPORT

CRITERIA TO APPLY FOR PERMANENT RESIDENCE (PR) OR CITIZENSHIP

After completing 5 years of uninterrupted stay in the country you can apply for both Permanent residence (PR) and a passport.

The difference between these two documents is:

Permanent residence:
1. You keep your original nationality
2. You cannot vote in national elections
3. Important change – once you get PR you do not need a sponsor anymore, hence if you (for example) lose your job, you can still stay in the country as long as you want to.
PR needs to be renewed every 5 years, but it is a relatively simple procedure.
Basically, it means that you can stay in the country without any reason like work or relationship.

Passport:

In this case, you become a citizen and enjoy all the rights of other citizens including voting rights, and visa-free travel where it is applicable.

In the Netherlands, you can submit your documents for a permanent residence by mail, and you have to apply for a passport in person at the city hall.

The list of documents is as follows:

· You must be 18 years or older.

· You can prove your identity and nationality with valid documents (your current passport).

· You have lived in the country for at least 5 consecutive years with a valid residence permit. You have always extended your residence permit on time. Importantly, you must have no gaps between your residence permits.

· At the time of your application for naturalization, you have one of the following residence permits:

- an asylum residence permit or regular permanent residence permit;

- a residence permit as a long-term EU resident;

- a temporary residence permit with a non-temporary purpose of stay;

- a resident permit as a family member of an EU national, if you yourself do not have the nationality of a country in the EU or EEA or Switzerland.

· On the date of the naturalization ceremony, you have a valid residence permit or you still have a valid right of residence under EU law. The naturalization ceremony is an opportunity for you and the municipality to jointly celebrate that you have obtained Dutch nationality.

PART VII: PERMANENT RESIDENCE OR PASSPORT

- You have passed the civic integration exam (see next chapter)
- You are not a danger to the public order or national security of the Kingdom of the Netherlands.
- You must renounce your current nationality. There are exemptions to this rule.
- You must be willing to make the declaration of solidarity during the naturalization ceremony. By making this declaration, you agree that the laws of the Kingdom of the Netherlands also apply to you.

Basically, it means that you must have the following:

1. Your current passport
2. Valid residence card (for at least one more year, because normally decisions about PR take up to 6 months and decisions about passports up to 1 year)
3. You must have stayed 5 years in the country without any gaps in your residence cards
4. You need to sign the declaration that you are willing to give up your current nationality
5. You must have a diploma to show that you passed the civic integration exams

Additionally, you need a copy of your birth certificate with apostille.

Suppose you already have all items except number 5, which you need to prepare in advance, let's say after staying in the country for about 4 years.

They can also ask about your employment contract (if you have a highly skilled migrant visa), your salary slips and your rental contract, but that is basically it.

The process of applying is very simple: you need to make an appointment, bring the documents, have a short conversation, normally in the local language, then they take your documents, you sign a couple of papers, pay, and then you are done. In NL the fee is around 900 euros for the passport. If they allow you to pay it means they accepted your documents and your applications. Prepare a couple of phrases to speak in the local language if you are not fluent, and at least know how to say "yes", because this is what you need to say the most during your appointment.

If another nationality gives you more options then take it, if not then do not take it. Nationality is a human invention; at the end of the day, we are all monkeys temporarily brought to this planet, so do not take yourself or your nationality too seriously. If it gives you more options then it is good, because it is always better to have more options. That's it.

INTEGRATION EXAMS

Integration exams mainly test your language skills on a very basic level plus your understanding of the country and society you are soon going to be part of.

In the Netherlands there are 5 main exams:

1. Reading
2. Listening
3. Speaking
4. Writing
5. Knowledge of Dutch society

You need to make an appointment for each exam, and you pay about 50 euros per exam.

You only get a diploma when you pass all 5 exams.

This diploma is what you need to bring with you when you apply for a passport.

You can take exams multiple times, but of course, each time you need to pay again.

Reading, Listening, knowledge of Dutch society, and part of the Speaking exam have videos or pieces of text and then multiple answers. Normally you can find sample exams online to get familiar with what it looks like.

Exams have a time limit, and you need to answer a certain number of questions to pass.

The second part of the speaking exam is where you actually need to speak to the microphone, and in the writing exam you have a piece of paper on which you need to write stuff.

Important points are:

1. Book your exams first, so you have a deadline to prepare for and motivation to study
2. You need to prepare to pass specific exams, not to learn the language with all its nuances.

Which means:

- Understand the structure of the exam, types of questions, and practice to answer them within the given time frame

- For writing and speaking exams, prepare a template of your answers. Do not add more words to your answer if they are not necessary. You only need to answer the question in a way that makes sense.

Mastering the language is a completely different story. Your immediate objective is to pass this specific exam, not to be knowledgeable on many topics that are unrelated to the exam.

The exam doesn't test your knowledge of the language in depth; the main point is to make sure that you can understand the context and can perform basic operations/interactions, and be self-sustainable.

You need to prepare FOR EXAMS, not just study Dutch. Exams test very basic knowledge and you need to do them in a timely manner. There is no grammar test or something like this, so there is no point spending years studying every grammatical rule. It is just about understanding the basics.

Step 1: Try test exams and see where you stand on each of them

Step 2: If there are gaps, find a crash course specifically preparing for integration exams. 1-2 weeks of intensive preparation is better than 6 months of studying something you probably do not need.

After 4 years in the country, you are very likely to pass anyway, so you only need to get familiar with the exam structure, identify gaps and learn basic templates/sentences you might want to use for writing and speaking.

If you start 1 year before you actually apply for a passport then you have plenty of time to do a re-sit in case you fail some of them.

And remember, it is easy: they just test some basics. It is almost impossible to fail if you know what the exam looks like and have some nice templates ready.

It is more a formality than a real challenge.

PREPARING THE DOCUMENTS

Well, the list of documents is very simple.

You just need to do integration exams in advance and also ask somebody in your home country to arrange a copy of your birth certificate with apostille, including translation to the local language verified by the notary, so the name in your passport will be exactly as it is on your birth certificate.

Again, the list of documents is:

1. Your current passport – you have it anyway, so there is nothing to prepare.
2. Valid residence card (for at least one more year, because normally a decision about PR takes up to 6 months and a decision about a passport up to 1 year) – you also have it.
3. You must have stayed 5 years in the country without any gaps in your residence cards – nothing to prepare, as they already have all your data.
4. You need to sign the declaration that you are willing to give up your current nationality – you can sign it on the spot.
5. You must have a diploma that you passed civic integration exams – you need to do this in advance, let's say after somewhere between 3 and 4 years staying in the country.

They can also ask about your employment contract (if you have a highly-skilled migrant visa), your salary slips, your rental contract, etc. Normally you have all this stuff available; even if it is not mentioned in the list of documents, just bring it with you in case they ask for it. In my case, I had to email it later since I didn't have it with me and it was not on the list of documents, but they asked for it.

Just a side note: with more or less the same documents you can apply simultaneously for a passport and a permanent residence card. In the Netherlands, PR costs around 150 euros and a passport around 900 euros. PR normally takes less time and can be ready somewhere between 2-6 months, while a passport can take up to 1 year.

In my case I thought paying € 150 extra to have more security 6 or 8 months earlier was worth it, so I applied for both.

I applied for PR by sending documents by post to the Immigration office (probably you can also do it electronically), and I applied for a passport in my municipality.

PR was ready in 4-5 months, and the passport took exactly 1 year.

When you have PR you do not need a sponsor any more and nobody can kick you out of the country if you lose your job. When you get the passport you need to give back your PR, because then it is not needed any more. But I thought that 150 euros is not a big investment to feel secure earlier than in 1 year.

If you want to keep your current passport, PR is probably more than enough. Of course, you need visas when traveling outside the EU, but within the EU your life is not much different from the one of regular citizens.

PART VII: PERMANENT RESIDENCE OR PASSPORT

But if you want even more flexibility and are willing to give up your current passport, then it is also ok to apply for citizenship. At the end of the day, it is just a practical question. Choose whatever works best for you. And see you on this side very soon!

DECISION AND NATURALIZATION CEREMONY

It all depends on the country, but I will tell you how it works in NL.

In approximately one year you will receive a letter from the Immigration office with their decision.

If the decision is positive, then in another 3-4 weeks you will receive another letter saying that this decision has been signed by the king.

In another 3-4 weeks you will receive an invitation to attend the Naturalization ceremony.

The ceremony is very simple: you just need to show up, say a couple of words in the local language saying that you will comply with all the rules of the country. After that, they will give you a certificate and proclaim you a citizen of the country.

With this certificate, you can make an appointment in the municipality and apply for a passport and ID card. You need to bring a photo, certificate, your current residence card, and passport. They will take your residence card and give you a temporary paper. A passport can be ready in around 1 week.

Then you make another appointment to pick up your passport.

If you signed a declaration to give up your current citizenship, then you need to start the process in your consulate.

They will give you some time for it and send reminders about when they expect you to submit papers proving that you: a) started the process, and b) completed the process.

And then you are done.

PART VIII:
WHAT'S NEXT

NOW YOU ARE A EUROPEAN CITIZEN, WHAT'S NEXT?

Getting citizenship after living about 6 years in the country probably won't feel like a big deal. You will realize that you have already settled there, got used to everything, and what once was a dream doesn't make you too excited when it became a reality.

It is just the end of the chapter.

The best thing to do is probably to move somewhere else and do something else.

We have an opportunity to live several lives within one.

To do this we need to change one of the components:

- Where we live
- What we do
- Who we live our life with

To start a new life, you should ideally change at least one or two items in this short list.

For example, you can get out of a relationship that doesn't make you happy.

If you are happy in the relationship, then you can consider changing your location and what you do.

Maybe you want to start teaching yoga or surfing and living in Madeira.

Or moving to Asia and meeting somebody from a totally different continent and culture.

Or getting out of the corporate environment and starting your own business, working remotely from the place you like the most.

In 6-7 years, you will make another iteration and start another life.

But it is good to try to have several lives instead of just one unless you are really in love with it and it is so perfect that there is nothing to change.

Keep challenging your current life, asking: Is this what I really want? Is this what I enjoy the most? After moving from your home country and becoming a citizen of the EU you know that nothing is impossible, and only your own perception and "factory settings" of your brain set the limitations.

In a few billion years this planet or even this universe will disappear, and nothing will matter. But here and now you can make a story of your life more exciting, more meaningful, just by daring to take the next step and being brave. And hey, this world is safe enough, and not many things can go wrong, so the risk is really not that high. The only real risk is the time that is running.

The biggest regret is not taking a step, not trying, not jumping to reach your dream. It is ok to fail, but it is not ok not to try.

PART VIII: WHAT'S NEXT

Who knows what your life could be, how much meaning you could create, and how much happiness you could experience? You will only know it if you try, if you dare, if you change, if you look for something new, different, exciting, something which adds color to your days and makes you excited to wake up and live.

And there are many people who are trying to do the same.

Be one of them.

We all can live many lives within one.

Find your next adventure.

And go for it!

SOURCES

Part 1, p. 17-24 (Hero's journey): Campbell, Joseph (2008). The Hero with a Thousand Faces (3rd ed.). Novato, CA: New World Library. ISBN 9781577315933.

Part 1, p. 17-24 Wikipedia (Hero's journey) https://en.wikipedia.org/wiki/Hero%27s_journey#CITEREFCampbell2008

Part 3, p. 54 FT ranking (official website)

Part 3 (p.41-51): Immigration and Naturalization Service website (The Netherlands)

Part 3 (p.57-64): Example from https://www.tias.edu/en/courses/mba/detail/fulltime-master-of-business-administration

Part 5, p. 119 "The almanac of Naval Ravikant", 2020

DISCLAIMER

This book is the author's perspective on the topic based on personal experience of living in the Netherlands. Situation and requirements can vary for different countries within the EU. Information is based on the author's experience and is not legal advice or guidance. For the most updated information please refer to official online sources.

Read and interpret generously. Original meaning can be different than your interpretation.

The provided information is not exhaustive, and its primary purpose is to inspire rather than to be a final source of truth. Please always check official documents of respective countries.

Printed in Great Britain
by Amazon